Merry & Chic

Merry & Chic

YOUR MOST DAZZLING CHRISTMAS EVER

Kathryn O'Shea-Evans

Gibbs Smith

First Edition
29 28 27 26 25   5 4 3 2 1

Text © 2025 Kathryn O'Shea-Evans

"Chocolate Cake with Whipped Cream" from *Audrey at Home* by Luca Dotti. Copyright © 2015 by Luca Dotti. Used by permission of HarperCollins Publishers.

All rights reserved. No part of this book may be reproduced by any means whatsoever without written permission from the publisher, except brief portions quoted for purpose of review. No part of this book may be used or reproduced in any manner for the purpose of training artificial intelligence technologies or systems.

Published by
Gibbs Smith
570 N. Sportsplex Dr.
Kaysville, Utah 84037

1.800.835.4993 orders
www.gibbs-smith.com

Designed by Amy Sly and Emily Austin, The Sly Studio
Art Director: Ryan Thomann
Editor: Juree Sondker
Production Designer: Brynn Evans
Production Manager: Felix Gregorio

Printed and bound in China

This product is made of FSC®-certified and other controlled material.

Library of Congress Control Number: 2024947875
ISBN: 978-1-4236-6848-0

For my beautiful mother, who can still hear the bell.

At Château du Grand-Lucé, designer Timothy Corrigan's former home in France's Loire Valley, he adorned a pine garland with "real mandarin oranges, miniature apples, and pinecones foraged from the woods" to add a festive air to the stone baluster.

CONTENTS

Introduction 8

01 / Wonderlands: Setting the Table 12

02 / The Most Magical Trees 50

03 / Deck Those Halls 80

04 / Darling for Darling: Children's Rooms 120

05 / Eat, Drink, and Be Merry, Merry: The Recipes 140

06 / Handmade, But Haute: DIY Gifts 184

07 / (Snow) Boot Camp 198

Acknowledgments 218

Buy Guide 221

Photo Credits 222

About the Author 224

INTROD

Why Your Christmas Obsession Is a Very Good Thing

I can admit when I have a problem. And I have a problem. I am a Christmas-aholic. The sparkle, the bows, the scent of just-trimmed evergreen boughs brought in from the cold . . . is there anything better? Especially when the sloshy, broody days of winter have darkened our doors for weeks on end?

Even in sunny Colorado, where I live with my husband and our young son, Guy, November and December are often among the dreariest days of the year. Yet during the Christmas season, everywhere there is an omnipresent feeling of lightness. The most septic of grocery stores smell of cinnamon. Offices shutter, inboxes lay un-pinged, and Slack finally lives up to its name. Strangers donate wish-list toys to children they don't know and will never meet. Fairy lights dot the landscape. And, of course, an ancient story is told again of a baby born with nothing—and everything. It's enough to make even the grinchiest of hearts triple in size.

I won't apologize for my obsession; I embrace it. In a country where freedom of belief is written into the Constitution, this is mine: Christmas is for anyone who wants to celebrate it. (Plus, despite our many differences, I've found that 99.89 percent of people like cookies and twinkle lights.) My love for the season can't be avoided. I grew up in a Christmas-loving family where holiday parties would stretch so late into the evening that I would fall asleep to the sound of giggles rising from the floor below like the heat of the fire.

Now that I'm a mother, the whole season has taken on a celestial importance. Something about "O Come Let Us Adore Him" hits differently when you're a parent. Every child on this earth deserves that adoration, if not the gold, frankincense, and myrrh. I start to decorate the second Halloween is over, and I favor natural or artisanal decorations over mass-produced flotsam (so much so that I even started my own little company, Aspen Grange, devoted to it). My husband, James, is the brawn, putting up twinkly lights with gusto. One year, he used a telescoping pole to hang lights on the twenty-five-foot-tall evergreen tree that stands in front of our house. When we lit it . . . a meteor shot across the sky like it was joining in the fun.

I originally wanted to title this book "Christmaspalooza," because to me that's what it is—a party when we need one most. More than that, whether you're sharing your holiday season with a flurry of extended relatives or alone in the city with your rescue pet, Christmas is love. I hope the designer ideas here make yours as love-bursting and holly-jolly as possible. Everything in here is eminently doable. As I wrote in my first book, I'm not a natural Martha and don't want anyone to feel stressed! Least of all, me. So I lean in to easy hacks and recipes that look a bit "wow" even when they're microwavable. (Don't believe me? See the "Christmas Confetti Chocolate Bark" on page 166.)

From my house to yours, merry merry! And may love and joy come to you.

Kathryn

ABOVE: The tulips of Spring can be Christmassy, too, especially in snow white (and paired with fresh persimmons), as Chandos Dodson Epley's Houston tablescape proves. Let them droop into a plié, as they were born to.

OPPOSITE: There's something about the drippy, asymmetrical placement of the bead garlands on Dodson Epley's tree that feels like Christmas at Mrs. Havisham's house, in the best possible way.

01/

WONDER- LANDS
SETTING THE TABLE

Let's get one important thing out of the way: you do not have to invest in a fleet of Ginori dinnerware to create a memorable night for your guests. Actually, some of my favorite holiday meals were served on paper plates. (My darling host was ninety-four and didn't want to do dishes. Who could blame her?)

—— EVEN ART DECO-ERA SOCIETY DECORATOR ELSIE DE WOLFE FAMOUSLY HELD RELAXED DINNERS ON TV TRAYS / THE IMPORTANT THING / AS MOST ANY NONAGENARIAN WILL TELL YOU . . .

IS TO ALL BE TOGETHER.

PREVIOUS: Custom touches can have a major impact. "We printed the place cards using an etching of the château and placed them in antique silver holders," says Corrigan, adding that the oval seating chart was hand carved by a master carpenter. "The linen place mats and napkins are embellished with a hand-embroidered pomegranate motif."

OPPOSITE: A mossy tablescape topping brings woodland decadence indoors. "With Christmas decor in general, I gravitate towards natural decorations," Tammy Connor says.

ABOVE: Like a fanciful bow, more is more when it comes to magnolia leaves, shown here dangling dreamily in Connor's office in a 1930s bungalow in Birmingham, AL.

That said, so much can be done to create a delightful table—and beautiful china is always appreciated. I love to begin with a hand-blocked tablecloth in rich hues that obscure those inevitable splotches and spills. Cotton and other natural fibers are best; eating is a primal moment, and a poly blend looks—and, more importantly, feels—off-putting to me.

WONDERLANDS: SETTING THE TABLE / 17

"I like simple, singular things grouped together versus an arrangement with a bunch of different flowers in it," Connor says, noting that mixing dainty paperwhites with herbs gives you varied textures that are all the more beautiful.

WONDERLANDS: SETTING THE TABLE

WONDERLANDS: SETTING THE TABLE / 19

OPPOSITE: Sky-high draperies and candelabras draw eyes up to the twenty-two-foot ceilings of the château, which feel especially grand at Christmas.

ABOVE: In his château, Corrigan employed soft salmon taper candles to complement the dining room's custom wall color. "The shade gives the room a rich, romantic glow, flatters people's complexions, and even makes the cuisine look more inviting," he says.

— WHOEVER SAID PERFECTION IS OVERRATED WAS TOTALLY RIGHT / SOMETIMES IT'S THE MISTAKES AND SNAFUS THAT MAKE A DINNER PARTY **MEMORABLE— AND FUN.**

PREVIOUS: "Portraits were selected to give the space a sense of formality and history," Corrigan says.

BELOW: Fresh persimmons from the autumn harvest were one muse for Chandos Dodson Epley's Houston tablescape. "I love incorporating magnolia, paperwhites, and tulips into my Christmas decor," she says of the fresh look.

RIGHT: Adorning the elegant silhouette of her dining chairs are "simple silk ribbon with magnolia, cedar, and glass ornaments," Dodson Epley says.

——— I LOVE TO BEGIN WITH A HAND-BLOCKED TABLECLOTH ———

IN RICH HUES...

Heather and Matt French of French & French enlisted Santa Fe's Renegade Floral to whip up three low arrangements tucked into wicker pedestal urns for the table with garden roses and evergreen. "We love incorporating natural materials like wicker to add warmth and texture," says Heather. "Using multiple smaller arrangements not only adds charm but also keeps the table practical—you can easily move them to the buffet or kitchen island during meals to make space for guests at the table."

Delicate stemware adds grace to a special moment. Water goblets should be sturdy, but for wine I seek out glasses so thin they could shatter if you look at them. You don't have to spend a lot; these can be found at resale shops, and mixing and mingling can have a very chic impact. My rule on investment silverware is that you have to hold it in your hands before you buy it. (It's sort of like those egg-shaped soaking tubs: some of them look cool, but get in and you'll find yourself unmoored, floating like a jellyfish!) In lieu of holding flatware in my hands before purchase, I scour eBay for big lots of affordable antique hotel, airline, or collegiate silverware. Thanks to the decades-old branding on the handle, they're always an instant conversation piece with a nice patina, and I love the memories I imagine they have of meals past.

ABOVE: Heirloom and borrowed tableware and custom monogrammed linens bring a sense of occasion to Virginia designer Ashley Hanley's tablescape. "My dear friend, KK Harris, is a talented calligrapher and helped write these menus for us," she says, noting that she added the blush-pink tassels (available at craft stores and on websites like Amazon) herself.

OPPOSITE AND FOLLOWING: Hanley transformed her husband's antique French desk into a bar for this soiree, using a mirror and garland to anchor the space. "I created various visual heights by including trays and books under decor and serving pieces," she says. "Instead of flowers, I wanted to keep this space feeling more masculine, so I opted for twigs of red berries that we pulled from our tree outside."

OPPOSITE: Sugared fresh cranberries and just-clipped evergreens bring some crispness to the table.

LEFT: "The secret to a great party punch is a beautiful punch bowl," says Aleah Valley of Seattle's Valley & Company Events. "We love to make an ice ring with frozen citrus inside from a mini bundt cake pan." And don't forget to add plenty of sparkling libations. "The fizzier the punch, the more festive!"

BELOW: "We dress up the stems of our etched glassware with velvet or plaid ribbon cinched in a bow for an extra dose of holiday cheer," Valley notes.

BELOW: For a recent holiday dinner in her circa 1880s New Orleans home, Katharine Kelly Rhudy of Reed & Acanthus created floral arrangements with some lively zing. "Rather than traditional Christmas green and red, the floral arrangements showcase tulips, ranunculus, hydrangeas, strawflowers, snapdragons, amaranths, and Arizona blue spruce," she says, noting that the mini splits of champagne she set beside each place setting was a fun way to get the evening started.

OPPOSITE: "For glassware, I prefer crystal rocks and highball glasses and plenty of martini or coup glasses for shaken drinks," Rhudy says of her home bar.

FOLLOWING: Connor spotted these carved wooden deer at an antique shop fifteen years ago, and they've graced her holiday tables with creature comfort ever since.

—— IT WAS CHRISTMAS WEEK / WE TOOK TO NO SETTLED EMPLOYMENT, BUT SPENT IT IN A SORT OF MERRY DOMESTIC DISSIPATION.
—CHARLOTTE BRONTË

It's fun to use an evocative item or two as a centerpiece, something Louisville, Kentucky–based designer Bethany Adams does beautifully. Take the fairy-tale-forest-inspired table she recently created for her family on pages 44–45. "I like to use whatever I have lying around to make a fantastic table and then top it off with some lovely flowers, and that's exactly what I did here," Adams says. "I do a fair amount of plant potting and had a bunch of this dried moss in a bin along with these darling—but outrageously heavy!—concrete mushrooms that are actually garden ornaments. (They are so heavy, I actually used a few for ballast on the large greenery installation on the mantelpiece behind the dining table after it completely fell onto the floor on my first try!) Back at the table, I clipped branches from our own magnolia tree, added some colorful tapers and the store-bought flowers, and the magical woodland came to life. The plates I used here were my paternal grandmother's. She had surprisingly modern taste. The pattern is 'Tumbling Leaves' by Royal Doulton, and the pretty foliage in browns and soft burgundies really inspired the whole table."

ABOVE: "A collection of sterling shakers is not only functional but an elegant touch to any bar," Rhudy notes. "Add a framed print, stylish tray, and monogrammed cloth cocktail napkins for a more personal touch."

OPPOSITE: Even small doses of greenery can bring so much life into a space at the holidays, as these chairback wreaths, tabletop topiaries, and cuttings on the chandelier by Maggie Griffin Design attest.

FOLLOWING PAGES: Madcap Cottage's dining room was inspired by the bar at the Gritti Palace in Venice, Italy—complete with a murano glass chandelier and peach silk drapery. "The table is huge—five feet wide—and it needed something substantial to anchor it," says John Loecke of the tree that graces the center.

CREATING AN
UNEXPECTED TABLESCAPE

◆

The best events are made more memorable—and hysterical—by those inevitable little slip-ups and shock moments. Case in point: During a 1929 Christmas Eve party at the White House, a blaze started in the attic and quickly spread. President Herbert Hoover determined that everyone could still have a good time safely, so the soiree continued—with plenty to talk about—as the firemen worked to snuff it out. (The next year, he cheekily gifted the children attending a toy firetruck.)

Certainly it's the blunders that can help everyone relax and laugh . . . which is hard to do if a pressed-linen host is frosty toward the guest that shows up with an avocado pie and frantic with worry about potential spills or broken china. One way to get the same calming effect as a bungle without hair-pulling is to place something unexpected or downright comical on your table. (Floral designer, author, and illustrator Cathy Graham is a wizard at this, adding things such as ceramic peas or gumdrops under drippy floral arrangements.) You could try a lush terrarium or a parade of snow globes or vintage toys fringed by battery-powered twinkle lights. Anything to put a smile on while lights are low.

OPPOSITE: "Varying the tapers and heights gives the tablescape so much more interest and movement and dimension, especially against the subtle mossy backdrop," Bethany Adams notes. "Also, most of us only have candlesticks in pairs, so for a big tablescape like this, you absolutely must use several different sets."

ABOVE: Adams created a woodland scene on her Louisville tabletop with concrete garden mushrooms and even mushrooms meant for fish tanks. Over a durable table runner, "I unrolled and trimmed a roll of moss matting from the craft store as a base, before filling it in with my decor and some looser bits of preserved moss to give it dimension," she says.

Elf, Shmelf

My former shrink had a joke about the "International Convention for Perfect Families"—there was nobody there, just a bunch of empty seats. Similarly, flaws are an inevitable part of Christmas, to be as expected as late deliveries. We're all on the island of misfit toys! What's truly important is not an Instagrammable table but giving people you love a great time while kicking up the beauty just a bit from everyday life. The reality is that showing up for the holidays and making memories with your loved ones—or just yourself—is the best gift of all . . . so don't waste one second worrying about a collapsed souffle. No one will notice; just pour another round of nog.

So, no, you don't *need* to do The Elf on the Shelf, that relatively new pixie that "shows up" every day in a different part of your house, often bearing gifts. A woman once told me she stays up late, pulling her hair out to plan her elf's brigades. More power to you if you genuinely want to do that, but I am not going to lose sleep over it. I feel your Christmas traditions will mean more if they come straight from you and your family. You could, for example, create a "gratitude tree" where instead of painstakingly sourcing miniature gifts for an Advent calendar, each day everyone in the house writes something they're thankful for on a paper "ornament" to hang on the branches. Or do what our son came up with recently—Fancy Fridays—where every Friday night you break out the good china, candles, and linens for dinner at home. That's more special-feeling to me than a pressure-cooker "tradition" could ever be, and it serves our family better—the less I have on my plate, the happier I am. (Unless it's a full plate of cookies, obviously.)

OPPOSITE: The most eye-catching tipples take center stage in Scott Francis and Mike Fabbri's New York City home bar. "The more impactful bottles—the European scotches and French liqueurs—stand out," he says.

FOLLOWING: A sterling silver trumpet vase corrals a burst of magnolia leaves, juxtaposed beautifully against a custom table skirt that Francis had made from tartan he imported from Scotland. "I've always loved the drama of a skirted tablecloth, especially on a round table," he says.

02/

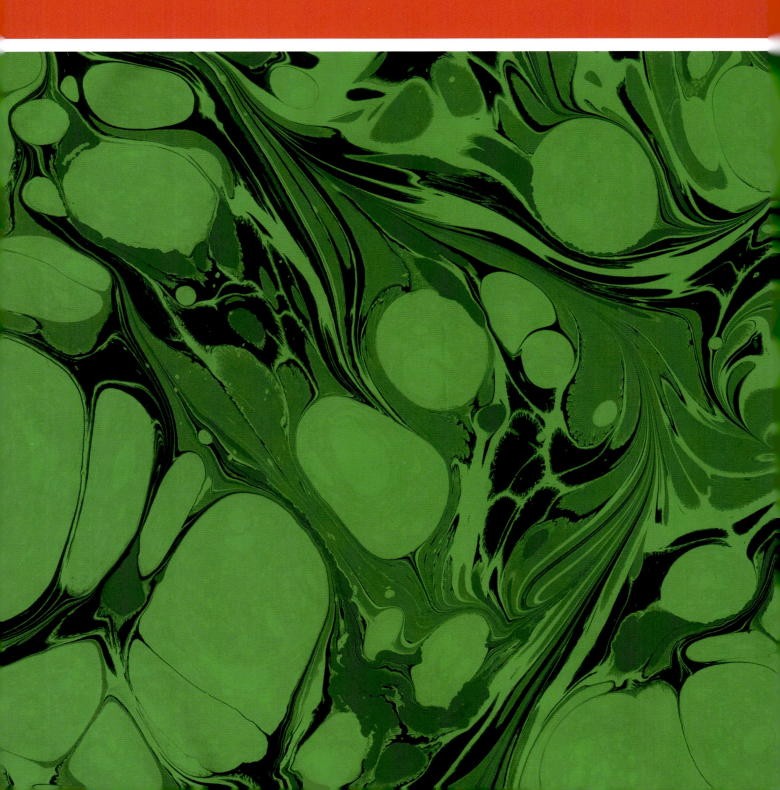

THE MOST MAGICAL TREES

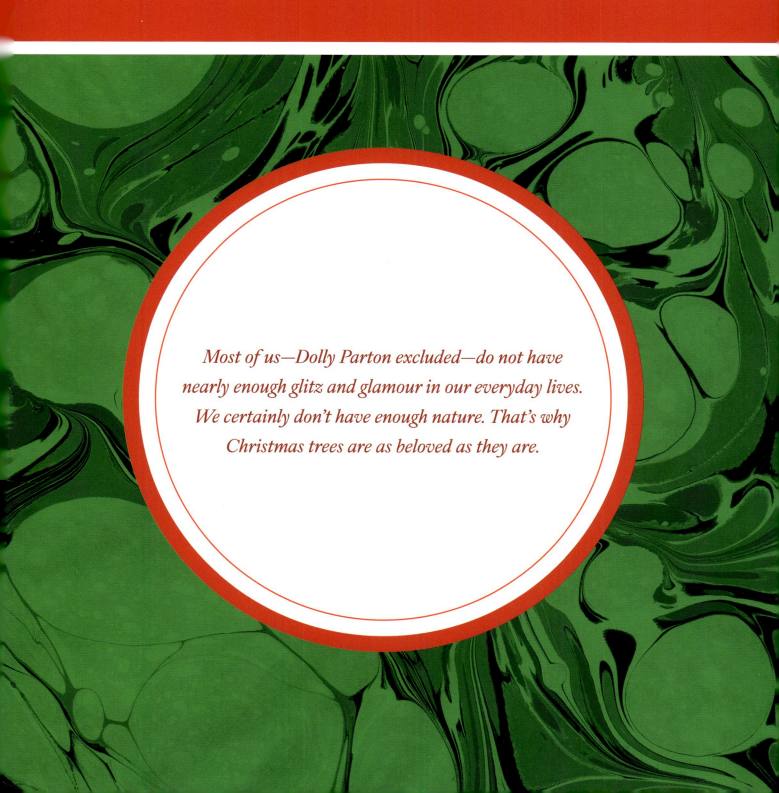

Most of us—Dolly Parton excluded—do not have nearly enough glitz and glamour in our everyday lives. We certainly don't have enough nature. That's why Christmas trees are as beloved as they are.

—— PICTURE IT / THE YEAR IS CIRCA 1500 / A WHIRLING SNOW HAS DESCENDED ON YOUR COPSE IN THE HINTERLANDS OF GERMANY / SOMEONE SAYS . . .

"LET'S GO CUT DOWN A TREE & BRING IT IN."

PREVIOUS: "I knew I wanted something a little over-the-top in our living room," Brittany Sydnor says of the tree in her 1926 Colonial in Lynchburg, Virginia. "I layered as many ornaments as the branches would support—at least a thousand—and vintage tinsel from an estate sale." Draped chiffon ribbons supply the final candy. "We named the tree 'Drippy,' which felt right," she says.

OPPOSITE: "I have been collecting large vintage brass deer for many years, and I loved the idea of creating a calm woodland scene around them instead of a more traditional 'Christmas-y' look," Adams says. "My daughter and I strung dried citrus slices on silk ribbons to make the garlands, which smell amazing."

FOLLOWING: Symmetrical magnolia garlands make for an especially grand entrance to Connor's Birmingham office.

It probably seemed insane, until it didn't. Shutters drawn shut to the elements, soot on every surface—seeing brilliant green needles must have been such a hopeful sight that it caught on. You could argue that the "Christmas tree" began when the sixteenth-century reformer Martin Luther reportedly added candles to his tree, wanting to bring the stars above indoors for his children. It was the earnest opposite of a dad joke—it was a dad delight.

Hundreds of years later, the Christmas tree has held up. We owe part of the tradition's longevity to royalty. (The press depicted Queen Victoria and Prince Albert decorating one in 1848, which popularized the concept. Who hasn't wanted something of Kate Middleton's for themselves?) There is something lovely about welcoming a standing Douglas fir or Scotch pine into your living room. I'm a purist, but there's absolutely no shame whatsoever in the faux versions, which seem to get more real-looking with every passing year and—if you have a high-end one you'll use for decades—are arguably more environmentally friendly in the long term. Just cut a few branches from your garden evergreens to stick in for scent.

James and I have embraced a tradition since we were newlyweds: every ornament on our tree is from a trip we've taken. Every year as we unwrap and hang them, the memories of those travels are a gift. The key to making a hodgepodge of baubles look chic is to add unifying balls in a singular color or two (I love a kelly green) and weave in some bows or ribbons—the wired versions are easiest to

—— AT CHRISTMAS EVERYBODY INVITES THEIR FRIENDS ABOUT THEM, AND PEOPLE THINK LITTLE OF EVEN THE WORST WEATHER.

—JANE AUSTEN

PREVIOUS: More is more at Christmastime in Paris. I love how the ball ornaments on these trailing garlands are concentrated at the top in different sizes, making them look like they drifted in on a breeze off the Seine.

OPPOSITE: Madcap Cottage maximized a foyer without much natural light by having every inch hand-painted, down to a Greek Key runner on the wood floors. The tree is tucked within a French garden planter, which "brings the outdoors in," Loecke says.

LEFT AND BELOW: The duo behind Madcap Cottage change up their holiday decor annually. "Tissue paper honeycomb ornaments are unexpected and in colors pulled from the painted scene on the wall," Loecke says.

THE MOST MAGICAL TREES / **61**

"One of the best parts of Christmas is collecting memories," says Loecke, co-founder of Madcap Cottage. "This flocked tree is basically a collection of ornaments from our childhoods and the places we've been."

mold into place. "We don't do a 'themed' tree at our house—my husband and I are both super sentimental, so you will find everything from his great-grandmother's old wooden spoons to the birth announcement of our goddaughter, and lots of handmade ornaments from our nieces and nephews or our childhood," says the Little Rock, Arkansas–based event and interior designer Jonathan Parkey. "I love how the concentration of bows gives an overall cohesive feeling, while the ornaments are so individual and not uniform."

If you prefer something more curated, you could do as Jacqueline Kennedy did when she was First Lady and embrace a singular motif (a White House tradition that began in 1961 when she used Tchaikovsky's *The Nutcracker* as her muse). The girl loved elegance! She also had a heart, investing in straw ornaments made by senior and disabled artisans to hang on the children's tree in 1962. Above all, go for what feels delightful to you. If your tree brings joy to you and yours, that's really all that matters.

ABOVE: "Tami, my mother and design business partner, collects Christopher Radko Santa ornaments for her tree," says Brelan Owen Pearson of The Owen Group. "Every year my mom gets a new one and continues to add to it. My grandfather used to give one to my mom every year, so they hold special memories."

OPPOSITE: "Since the entire tree is Santa themed, we stick to big bow toppers," Owen Pearson says. "We make the bows for our clients' too. It adds a nice touch to pull the ribbon through the tree for an interest and continuity."

FOLLOWING: Designer Gray Walker's North Carolina living room is an ode to holiday maximalism, complete with a magnolia garland intertwined with cuttings from her own garden. "I love an old fashioned Christmas tree," she says. "I collect vintage ornaments all year long! The finishing touches in creating this look are strands of gold balls and loads of tinsel aesthetically dripped and draped over the tips of the tree branches." Colored Christmas lights and needlepoint stockings complete the throwback aesthetic.

COCKTAIL PARTY
PLAYLIST

◆

"Santa Baby" will always be tinsely gold, but these songs are just as merry and bright:

"Linus and Lucy"–Vince Guaraldi Trio

"Just Like Christmas"–Low

"Back Door Santa"–Clarence Carter

"A Christmas to Remember"–Dolly Parton and Kenny Rogers

"Christmas Is"–Lou Rawls

"Spotlight on Christmas"–Rufus Wainwright

"That's Christmas to Me"–Pentatonix

"'Zat You, Santa Claus?"–Louis Armstrong

— TO GET THE FULL VALUE OF JOY YOU MUST HAVE SOMEONE TO DIVIDE IT WITH.

—MARK TWAIN

Skip the Gifts

PREVIOUS: Dallas designer Denise McGaha wove various types of foliage throughout her clients' mantel-top garland for rich texture that reflects the sumptuous space.

OPPOSITE: Muted grays and glimmering golds in the bows on this garland in Rhudy's circa 1880s New Orleans home echo the palette in the scenic wall mural at left.

Yes, *of course* I want the 8.24-carat ruby and diamond Van Cleef & Arpels ring that Richard Burton gave to Elizabeth Taylor, hiding it deep in the bottom of her stocking on Christmas Day in 1968. (She screamed.) But some of my very best Christmases at our house happened when our gifts weren't even gifts. They were plane tickets and hotel bookings and restaurant reservations: in Rome, in Iceland, in South Africa. I really, truly do *not* need any more shoes! And neither do you, probably.

OPPOSITE: Soft blues and glimmering silvers give Tuft & Trim designer Courtney Davey's tree the appeal of a bluebird ski day. Loose, dangly ribbons lend a casual look that helps guests feel at home.

ABOVE: Plaids and more plaids on Davey's presents give them a tailored impact, especially handsome in shades of green and blue.

ABOVE: "I think it is important for your tree to be in context to what is happening with the rest of the home, staying in the same 'vocabulary,' so to speak," says Dodson Epley. "My house is mid-century, so I love the different shapes of some of my blown-glass ornaments in bronze and pearl. We used glass beads instead of ribbon this year and added some blown-glass green ornaments for a pop of rich colors."

OPPOSITE: Under a vintage steel and brass convex mirror, "The mantel is fresh garland mixed with magnolia and blown-glass ornaments," the designer says. "I love using magnolia because it works so well in our warm Houston climate at the holidays." Her maltese, Gigi, takes in the scene.

OPPOSITE: Hanley employs sentimental ornaments first, before filling in the gaps with decorative ones. "My very last layer (and my husband's least favorite!) is old school tinsel," she says. "It adds the most beautiful sparkle to the tree that I absolutely love."

ABOVE: "Growing up, my grandmother had a new theme every year for her tree decor, and I find myself subconsciously doing this with my gift wrap every year," Hanley says. The tree skirt is custom; the designer had it made at her sewing workroom with leftover Quadrille fabric from her throw pillows, and Schumacher chintz.

So while children can and should be treated to baubles and books and a new trinket or toy (or ten!) at Christmas, it can be fun and transportive to put added emphasis on an experience, especially for teens and adults. It doesn't have to be travel. Maybe it's a rollicking game night every Friday during the Christmas season. Maybe it's volunteering at your local soup kitchen as a family, caroling in a nearby eldercare facility, or taking nature walks in enchanted woodlands to clear the holiday air. Embrace the intangible magic over the commercial and you may find that your Christmas experience is even richer, no rubies required.

03/

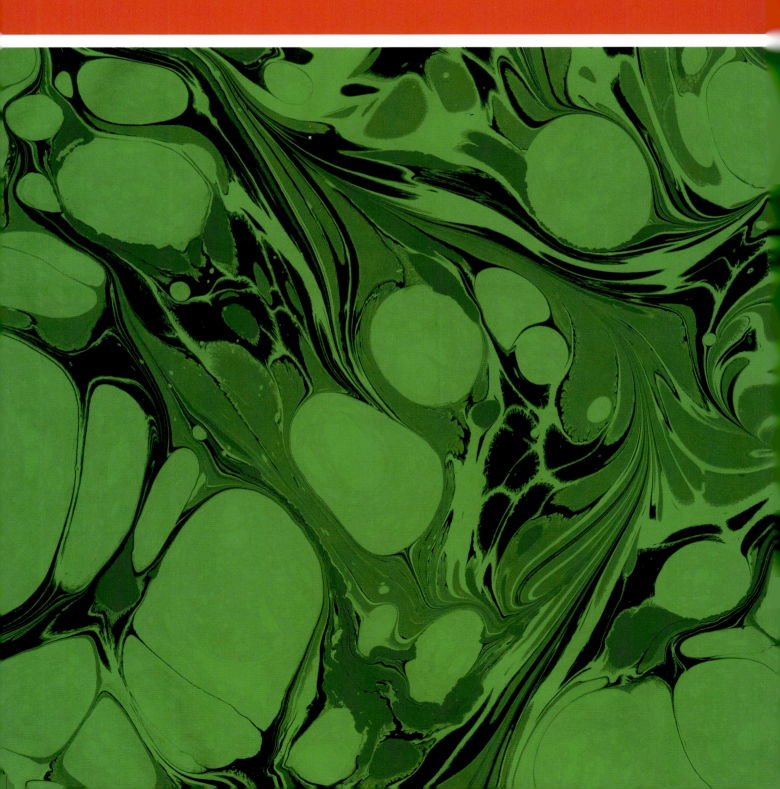

DECK THOSE HALLS

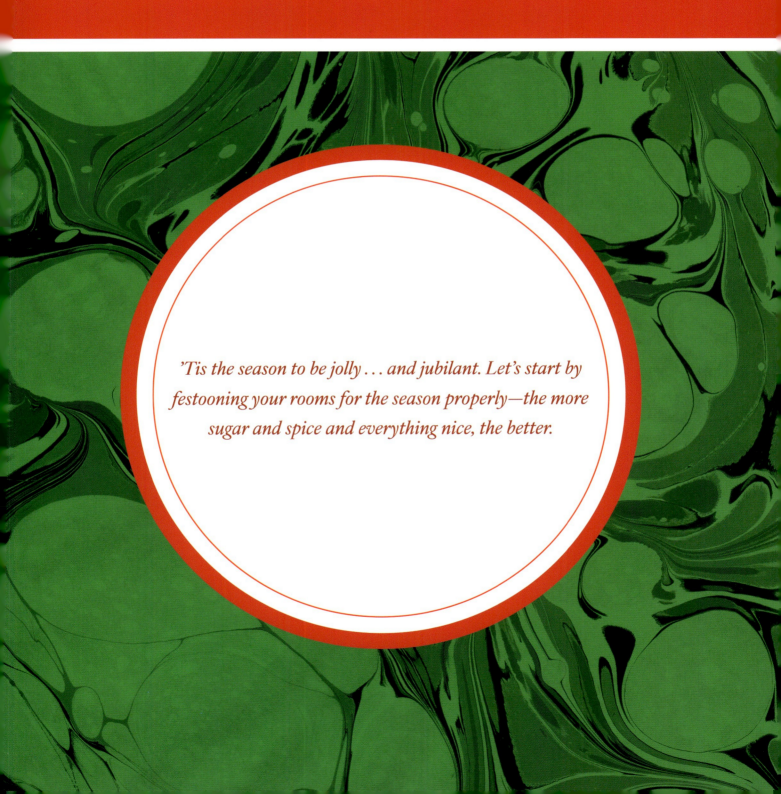

'Tis the season to be jolly... and jubilant. Let's start by festooning your rooms for the season properly—the more sugar and spice and everything nice, the better.

—— THE FEELING MANY PEOPLE GET WHEN THEY LEAVE A SALON WITH GREAT HAIR? / THAT'S HOW CHRISTMAS OBSESSIVES FEEL

WHEN THE HALLS ARE BEAUTIFULLY ADORNED.

PREVIOUS: Corrigan's garlands in France are bedecked with the fruits of nature.

OPPOSITE: A trio of wreaths adorn the windows of Sydnor's Virginia sunroom, where she cut the legs off the sofa so it would tuck perfectly below the sill. Red window muntins add to the decadent aesthetic.

It's like you're wearing your gladdest glad rags every single time you pass by. No studio rental apartment or sprawling estate can't benefit from a dusting of merriment.

Faux garlands and boughs are a great starting place, and you can use them for decades... but none have yet to replicate the whiff of just-cut evergreen. So once I've anchored my boughs using adhesive hooks (just as effective on a horizontal surface), I zhush my decking by grabbing the gardening shears and heading outside, where juniper and blue spruce trees await, ripe for the plucking. Cut branches fresh and weave them in with the faux stuff. The occasional dust-bustering of needles is worth it for the herbaceous scent. Into all that woodland wonder I'll add pine cones my son and I find on our walks, some metallic ornaments and sheen-y ribbons for glam, and of course a dusting of twinkly lights on a timer—so they'll be waiting, turned on in all their glory, when we get home from the day.

Keeping to one cohesive color palette makes things a bit easier, but a layered one can be more transfixing. Hues you spot on a nature hike will always work together—sky blues and forest greens; emeralds and buffaloberry red; sage and the camel brown of the trail itself. Parkey unifies his mantel with the rest of the room's color palette; he had custom stockings made from the same fabric that upholsters the nearby formal dining room. "I then hand embroidered them with our names—even giving one to our adorable boxer, Judy," he says. "I also did a DIY stocking holder, spray-painting wooden nutcrackers to make them feel more modern and slick." Classic yet modern mission accomplished—see page 105!

ABOVE: A flurry of evergreen wreaths and garlands can be all you need for an impactful Christmas statement, as these interiors by Los Angeles event designer Beth Helmstetter can attest.

OPPOSITE: The already abundant charms of a canopy bed get a boost of hygge with a simple wreath, tied with ribbons and bells.

OPPOSITE: Helmstetter accentuates the graceful lines of a burl wood secretary desk with a loose garland, tied with scarlet and evergreen bows.

LEFT: The graphic beauty of a tableware collection has a dusting of pixie dust with Helmstetter's lit garland.

BELOW: Bijou trees and wreaths transform a corner reading table into a moment of holiday delight.

DECK THOSE HALLS / **89**

ABOVE: If Jackson Pollock had a line of wrapping paper, it might look something like these beauties by Utah designer and color wizard Hillary Taylor.

OPPOSITE: In limiting the color palette to shades of blue and green, Taylor set a calming holiday scene inspired by the natural world. The fringed table skirt and ribbons around the chair legs supply the grace of a ballerina.

ABOVE: Consider rich red and pink taper candles to bring transfixing drama, as Adams did, in lieu of ho-hum white or cream. "Mix them up, use different candles to complement your room's decor, and the effect will be stunning," she says.

OPPOSITE: To get this look on her circa 1897 stair rail, Adams swagged ready-made live garland starting at the top of the banister using plastic zip ties. "At every zip tie location, we tied an enormous satin bow (eight or nine inches wide), then cut the ends of the ribbon on the diagonal," she says. "Truly nothing could be simpler and have a more stunning effect."

FOLLOWING: "The wreaths hanging in our family room windows are preserved boxwood, so that we can reuse them year after year," Hanley says. "Every time we take them down after the holidays, our windows always feel so empty without them!"

On her stair rail, Adams prefers to begin with the real stuff rather than faux, and she keeps it simple by design. "It is actually quite a struggle to hang a living garland in the first place, so ladening it with decor is both overwhelming and unnecessary," she says. "I used a spool of eight- or nine-inch-wide satin craft ribbon, and my twelve-year-old daughter and I tied bows around every spot where the garland was zip-tied to the banister. The bonus is that it was incredibly easy to undecorate after the holidays, and those ribbons are stored safely for next year."

OPPOSITE, ABOVE RIGHT, AND BELOW: "The little touches of ribbon, candy canes, sprigs of preserved boxwood add just the right amount of festive feel in our home," says Hanley. "It helps highlight my collections and my beautiful antiques."

ABOVE LEFT: A ribboned garland serves as a backdrop for holiday cards in Hanley's home. "We make sure to keep a box of paper clips and extra ribbon nearby to add to our garland for displaying the cards."

One of the best Christmas decorating tips you'll ever hear is also the easiest: let your hair down a little bit! Fill a bowl with ornaments that could be considered twee; swap the hand towels for the frankly inelegant ones that kids gravitate to. "The hardest thing for me about holiday decorating is letting loose and having fun," Parkey admits. "I've learned to try to let go of the more serious way in which I approach decoration and lean into the whimsy and magic of the season.... I mean, sometimes something a little tacky is exactly what you need to finish off the space." They go for over-the-top abundant greenery at their entrance: "We usually go to our friend Meredith's house and cut down as much magnolia from her backyard as she allows us. We then layer it in—sort of like our table arrangements with color and texture—spraying some of the magnolia with gold spray paint for texture and sparkle. I always love going for a lush and layered look."

ABOVE: "After decorating the main trees, I had a few leftover vintage silver and blue ornaments," Sydnor recalls. "Not one to leave an ornament behind, I grabbed a small tabletop tree from the nursery down the street and decided the pantry was the perfect spot for it. It's open to our mudroom, where we come and go every day, so it's a lovely little holiday surprise just a few steps into the house."

OPPOSITE: Any empty bowl or hurricane vase is an opportunity for a de facto firework of ornaments, as Sydnor proves.

OPPOSITE: Atop a nineteenth-century Louis Phillip Walnut chest of drawers with bronze hardware, Dodson Epley placed paperwhites and an entrancing present. "I love wire ribbon because they make the most beautiful bows that stay intact," she says. "You can reuse it for years."

ABOVE: A faux garland is practically required in the Texas climate, but Dodson Epley wove in fresh sprigs of magnolia for texture. Opaque and clear glass orbs suit her 1964 home perfectly.

FOLLOWING: Madcap Cottage recreated a mirror from England's circa 1660 Badminton House to add height to their home's existing mantel. At the holidays, it gets an especially festive layer of glimmering decor.

—— I WILL HONOUR CHRISTMAS IN MY HEART, AND TRY TO KEEP IT ALL THE YEAR.

—CHARLES DICKENS

ABOVE: A modern way to display collected ornaments: glass column vases filled to the brim with the baubles, as shown in Jonathan Parkey's Arkansas home.

OPPOSITE: "Holidays are always red for me," Parkey says. Here, a few well-placed bows and tassels do the trick . . . and add a punch alongside the natural cuttings.

Parkey's parties are also spectacularly unexpected, which is fitting at a time of year when one of the best things you can serve up is amazement. He and his family regularly host a holiday fête prior to the Christmas dance at his country club. "This is always in early December, so a great kickoff to the season. Because it's a pre-party and a fully coursed dinner will be served at the dance, we serve only French fries from our favorite neighborhood haunt, Cheers. Guests are greeted with a glass of champagne and a full formal dining table of French fries served on silver trays. We always have a full bar in our courtyard and golf-cart valet from our house to the country club. . . . I mean who doesn't love French fries and champagne?" I'd RSVP "Yes" every time.

OPPOSITE: Simple makes a statement in this bar by Maggie Griffin Design, where a diminutive rosemary topiary tied with a blue bow is all it takes to welcome the season.

ABOVE: Black ribbons can make the hues of vintage ornaments look even more rich (shown here: Valley's collected trinkets).

DECK THOSE HALLS / **107**

OPPOSITE: "Above the mantel in our front room, we used a citrus garland sourced from a local florist here in Santa Fe," says Heather French. "What we love about this is that it features not only oranges, but grapefruits and limes which gives it more of a unique touch."

ABOVE AND LEFT: The team behind French & French styled their antique armoire and sideboard with layers of evergreen, winterberries, and a selection of miniature village houses to set a wintry scene.

As a final touch in our suburban Colorado house, I whirl around like a sugarplum fairy with an easy upgrade—miniature wreaths looped over my arm to dispense. Thanks to the magic of adhesive hooks, you can pop them on mirror fronts, glass-fronted art pieces, even chairbacks. Add a flouncy bow and—poof!— you're done, doll. Time for some nog.

BELOW: Symmetrical garlands and topiaries bursting with fruit—a Christmas decor classic since the Colonial era—give Gray Walker's 1965 Charlotte, North Carolina Georgian Revival home an especially warm welcome. "Smilax, Korean fir, and Oriental bittersweet vines were added on my front porch," she says.

RIGHT: Wreaths slung over the wall sconces and ski-bunny throw pillows transform this alcove by Helmstetter into the ultimate reading nook.

FOLLOWING: Lacey, silvery foliage tucked into the garlands on Rhudy's circa 1880s stair rail in New Orleans mirror the flora in the scenic wall covering.

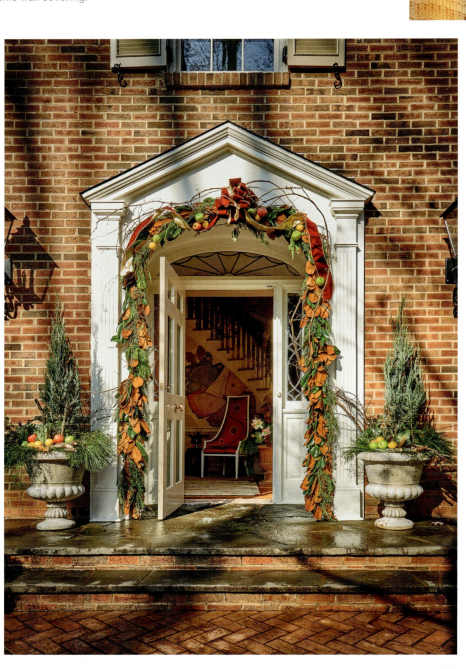

—— ISN'T IT A LOVELY CHRISTMAS? I'M SO GLAD IT'S WHITE. ANY OTHER KIND OF CHRISTMAS DOESN'T SEEM REAL, DOES IT?

—LUCY MAUD MONTGOMERY

CHRISTMAS EPISODES TO WRAP TO

◆

It's embarrassing, but the only way I can get through certain tasks is by having something to hold my hand: a sitcom I have seen umpteen times playing in the background. These are a few of my go-to holiday-related episodes. Not feeling it? Try a Hallmark movie; they're typically easy to follow without looking at the screen.

Frasier
"Frasier Grinch" (season 3, episode 9)
"High Holidays" (season 11, episode 11)

Friends
"The One with the Holiday Armadillo" (season 7, episode 10)

Gilmore Girls
"The Bracebridge Dinner" (season 2, episode 10)

Ted Lasso
"Carol of the Bells" (season 2, episode 4)

The Office (US)
"Christmas Party" (season 2, episode 10)
"Secret Santa" (season 6, episode 13)

Parks and Recreation
"Citizen Knope" (season 4, episode 10)

Seinfeld
"The Strike" (season 9, episode 10)

Will & Grace
"Jingle Bells" (season 4, episode 12)

The Truth about Santa

I think it's time we all admit the truth about Santa. *Mrs. Claus does everything.* Or at least quite a lot. She makes the list. She checks it twice. She wraps up the gifts for everyone, both naughty and nice. She probably feeds the reindeer, takes the sleigh into the shop, and doles out the holiday bonuses to the elves, too. But it's Santa who gets all the fanfare.

The data backs this up. According to a British study of couples by YouGov, 69 percent of women said they send out the holiday cards, versus 12 percent of men. And 61 percent of women buy the presents, versus 8 percent of men.

So, yes, I think Mrs. Claus does way more than she's given credit for. I'd wager that the big man does the icy driving and hangs the lights. That he hooves it down the chimneys, braving the break-and-enter. I just hope he remembers to bring home a cookie or two for his wife. And that when the second Sunday in May rolls around, he throws her a ticker-tape parade.

PREVIOUS: Hanley's ceiling sheathed in Schumacher's Florence Lapis wallpaper inspired the 3D paper stars, which she made by hand after watching a how-to video online.

OPPOSITE: What is an empty corner if not begging for a tree? A basket in lieu of a tree stand gives this darling one designed by Helmstetter an earthy, artisanal impact.

OPPOSITE: Candles in a window have been used since ancient times to symbolize welcome and hospitality. Here, Helmstetter added hurricanes for an old-world effect.

ABOVE: There's something about a full-length skirt on a round table that is as elegant as a holiday gala (here, Davey topped her table with plenty of greenery and flickering candles for added impact).

04/

DARLING FOR DARLING
CHILDREN'S ROOMS

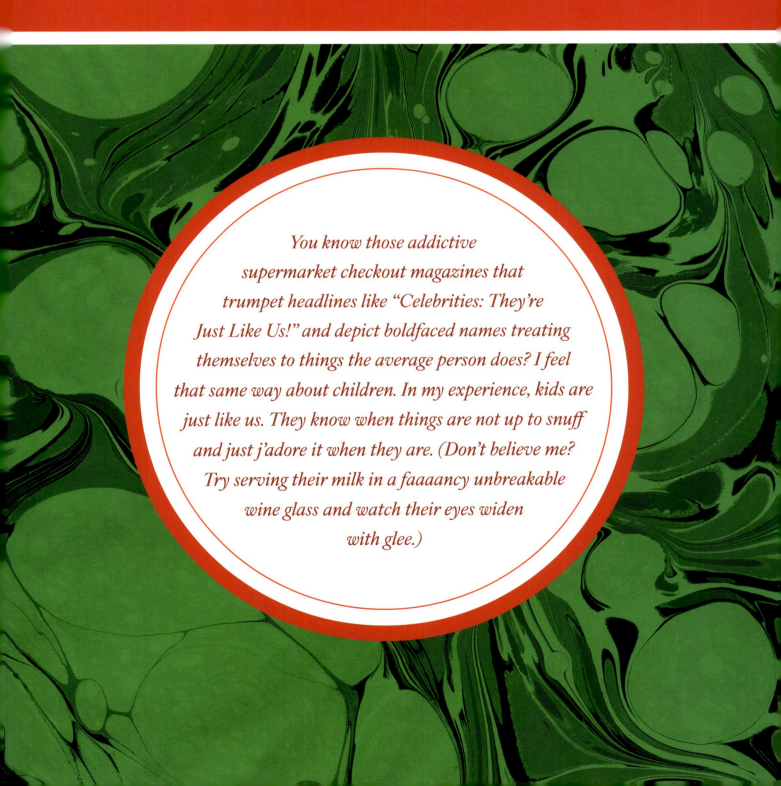

You know those addictive supermarket checkout magazines that trumpet headlines like "Celebrities: They're Just Like Us!" and depict boldfaced names treating themselves to things the average person does? I feel that same way about children. In my experience, kids are just like us. They know when things are not up to snuff and just j'adore it when they are. (Don't believe me? Try serving their milk in a faaaancy unbreakable wine glass and watch their eyes widen with glee.)

—— IN MY EXPERIENCE, KIDS ARE JUST LIKE US. / THEY KNOW WHEN THINGS ARE NOT UP TO SNUFF . . .

AND JUST J'ADORE IT WHEN THEY ARE.

PREVIOUS: In Sydnor's daughter's room, the chinoiserie wallpaper and pink chandelier inspired an equally ethereal Christmas tree—with soft pastel hues and occasional jewel tones for interest. "The delicate ornaments live closer to the top (if you get me) because my daughter, in particular, is known to 'redecorate' her tree throughout the season," she says.

OPPOSITE: A well-placed antique rug serves as a tree skirt in Sydnor's son's room, where the tree is decked in some of his favorite trimmings, including red yarn for a homey touch. "I suppose the romantic in me flashes forward to a time when they'll reminisce on the magic of the season and so I approached their rooms with that in mind," she says. "What does magic look like to a three- and eight-year-old? Your very own tree, of course!"

FOLLOWING: Cut paper angels grace the mantel of this child's room designed by Adams, where blush pink ribbons echo the tile on the hearth.

So, yes, kids deserve a beautiful bedroom when at all possible. That includes some festive touches just for the Christmas season. (Just make sure you're decking their li'l halls safely, in a childproof way—nobody wants a bough to fall on their head.) Hanging twinkle lights is an easy yet magical move; a garland over their windows feels sumptuous and royal. Kids who are old enough may appreciate a tree of their own that they can see as they're drifting off to dreamland; this is a great opportunity for them to decorate however they want in ways you may not love in your living room. Spiderman or Candyland theme? Neon ornaments? Go wild, sugar. Your room, your rules.

It sounds counterintuitive in a summer-obsessed culture, but winter is also one of the best seasons to be outside, creating kidsy mayhem in the frosty air. If your house is largely your domain, the landscape beyond your doors is theirs: with one foot in the wilder world yet simultaneously at home. So when it snows, take advantage. Bundle up in the warmest wools you can find and join them for snow-fort building, snowpeople making, and even a few snow cones. The only thing you'll regret is not joining them.

SNOWFLAKES & SURPRISES: TRADITIONS LITTLE ONES LOVE

◆

Get your tree in the forest. Given our teetering ceilings and proximity to the woods, our family tradition is to trudge into the mountain forest to cut down an enormous tree ourselves. (Colorado's Forest Service sells permits for twenty dollars, the best deal of the holiday.) The tree smells fantastic, is as organic as a rushing stream, and is so fresh that we once had one continue to grow, sending off bright green shoots. I think she was happy to be warm inside the house.

Ogle the lights. Once a season, our family dons our coziest pj's, picks up some drive-through cider with plenty of whipped cream, and takes in the magical light show springing up in our neighborhood. But the sun sets so early here that my son Guy and I also do the same thing just the two of us after school pickup, blasting classic Christmas music and weaving through the neighborhoods slowly, meanderingly—hunting for the most garish displays of holiday affection we can find. (Blow-up Christmas decor wasn't my thing until I had a child. Now it's nearly a reincarnation of Disney fun on any lackluster sidewalk.)

Build a holiday fort. Whether you set it up indoors with sheets and blankets or outside with ice blocks as snow whirls around you, there's nothing like a fort. Battery-operated twinkle lights and faux-fur blankets and pillows ensure that it's snuggle-ready in there.

DIY ornaments. Every year we pick up some simple brown papier-mâché ornaments at a local craft store and set up a painting party—razzle-dazzling each ornament before letting them dry, giving them a sheen with Mod Podge, and writing the year and the name of the artist in permanent marker on the back. These go on the kid tree, if Guy wants—and are a great reminder of family exploits.

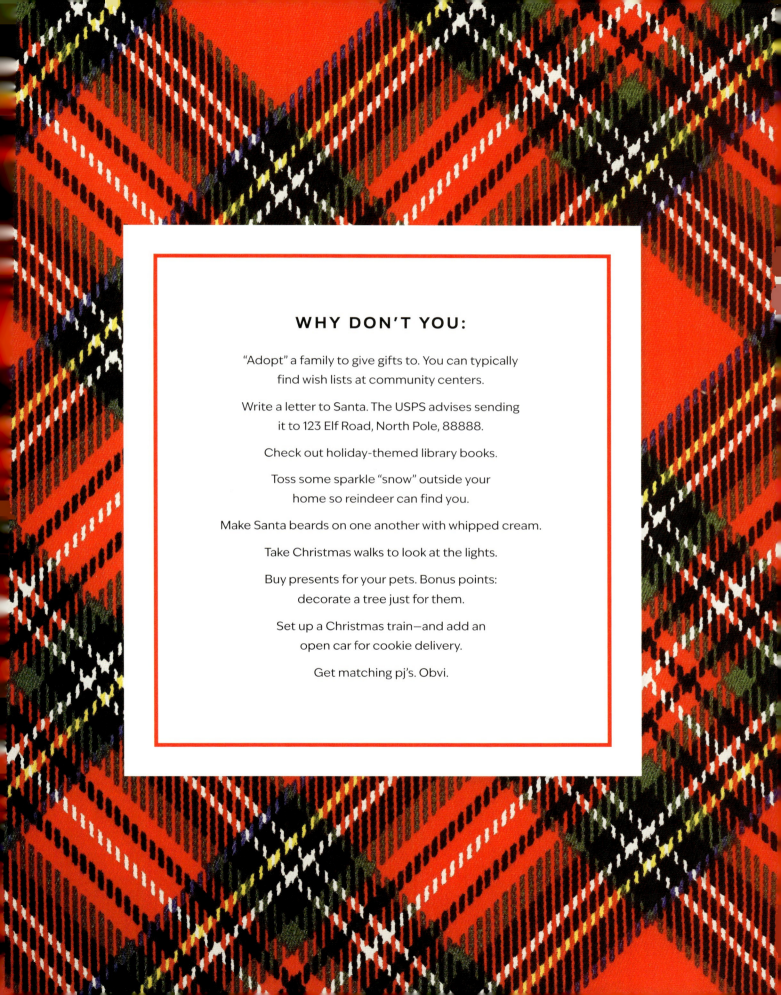

WHY DON'T YOU:

"Adopt" a family to give gifts to. You can typically find wish lists at community centers.

Write a letter to Santa. The USPS advises sending it to 123 Elf Road, North Pole, 88888.

Check out holiday-themed library books.

Toss some sparkle "snow" outside your home so reindeer can find you.

Make Santa beards on one another with whipped cream.

Take Christmas walks to look at the lights.

Buy presents for your pets. Bonus points: decorate a tree just for them.

Set up a Christmas train—and add an open car for cookie delivery.

Get matching pj's. Obvi.

In Praise of the Imperfect Christmas

One of my best Christmas memories is also my worst. In the year after our son, Guy, was born, I was a new mother determined to create The Perfect Christmas for our Perfect Son. It was peak COVID-19 then, and we would be spending it alone in our home, our families more than a thousand dreary miles away. What could make this better? "A-ha!" I thought. "I'll stock up on delectable 'treat' foods and premade meals I just have to pop in the oven."

Well, I did. And then something went really horribly, horrifically wrong. I don't know what we ate that did it, but in came the most wicked snurricane of food poisoning that had ever hit my husband. I very cavalierly announced, "I feel fine!" popped Guy in the stroller, and went for a walk in the crisp alpine air. And then . . . I did not feel fine.

"As my kids are getting older, I am letting them start to decorate their own mini trees and their rooms with miscellaneous decor," Hanley says. "They cannot wait to get their supplies out of the holiday bin to start decorating!" The wicker reindeer were a find at a local antique shop.

DARLING FOR DARLING: CHILDREN'S ROOMS

ABOVE: The littlest of littles might enjoy a teensy tree, as Adams has placed here—and you'll sleep better knowing it's set high out of reach.

OPPOSITE: Helmstetter hid a wreath within this canopy bed, and garlands along the rail, for an unexpected dose of evergreen grandeur.

—— AND WHEN THEY WENT AWAY, LEAVING COMFORT BEHIND, I THINK THERE WERE NOT IN ALL THE CITY FOUR MERRIER PEOPLE THAN THE HUNGRY LITTLE GIRLS WHO GAVE AWAY THEIR BREAKFASTS AND CONTENTED THEMSELVES WITH BREAD AND MILK ON CHRISTMAS MORNING.

—LOUISA MAY ALCOTT

PREVIOUS: Red and white stripes are forever Christmassy...and forever classic.

OPPOSITE AND ABOVE: DIY garlands of paper pennants and homespun ornaments add a touch of childhood's eternal joys to this tree. A smattering of well-placed deer ornaments give it some glimmer.

We'd been so careful and lucky to not have COVID, and then there we were, a scene from *Bridesmaids*... while our nearly one-year-old (who thankfully had his own *bébé* diet and hadn't tried the poison) looked on, very likely wishing he was away in a manger.

Now I look back on our first Christmas as a family of three and not only giggle but think how nice it was that we were there together, wiping each other's brows and serving up restorative liquids. And Guy loved it. We weren't rushing about but on the floor with him (albeit in a less-than-perfect state). He still loves the toy he got that day—a Vermont-made teddy bear—and laughs. "That was the Christmas Mommy got sick on the floor!" And we laugh too. So now my Christmas motto is to embrace the flaws. Gifts didn't arrive in time? Use it as an excuse to extend the magic. Stores had a run on cranberry sauce? Try to concoct your own raspberry sauce instead. And go ahead and let those berries grind stains into the marble without a worry. When you see them, all you'll hear is laughter.

ABOVE: Simple decorations can go a long way in children's rooms: garlands of paper stars, a hand-carved wood rocking horse brought in for the season.

OPPOSITE: Catherine Olasky adorned this little girl's room with a heart-shaped magnolia wreath.

05/

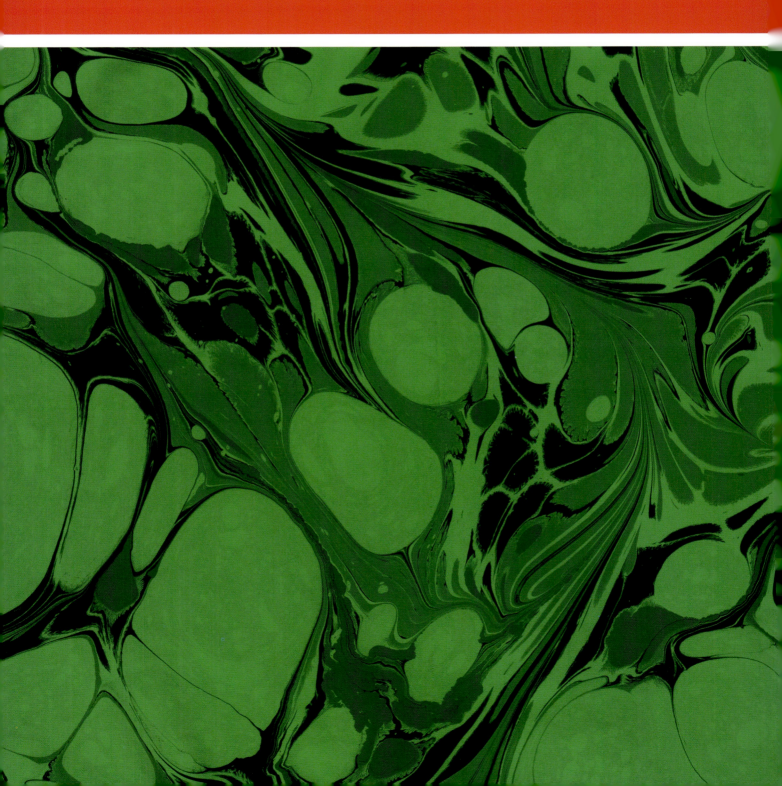

EAT, DRINK, AND BE MERRY, MERRY
THE RECIPES

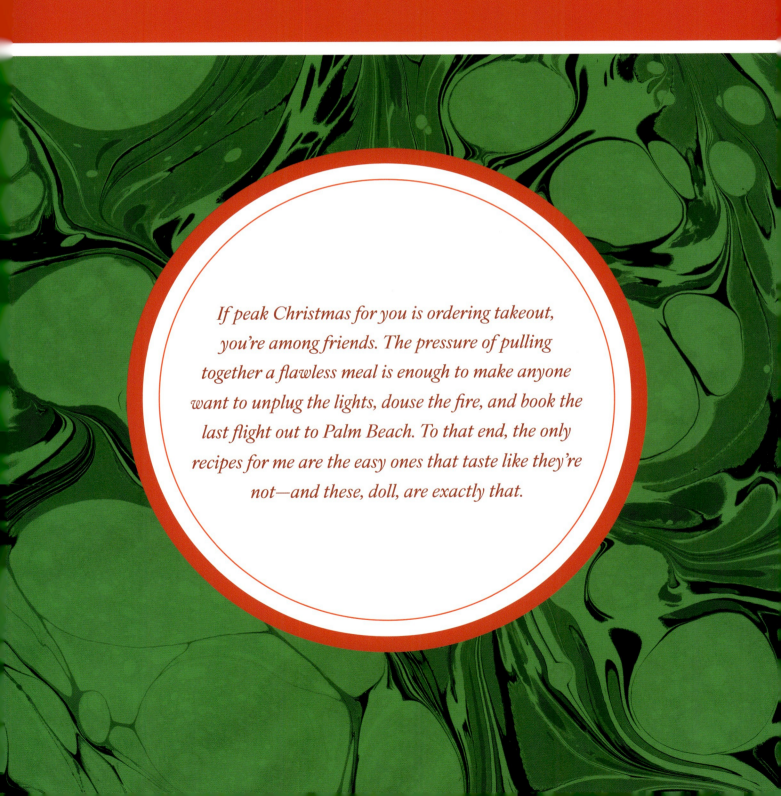

If peak Christmas for you is ordering takeout, you're among friends. The pressure of pulling together a flawless meal is enough to make anyone want to unplug the lights, douse the fire, and book the last flight out to Palm Beach. To that end, the only recipes for me are the easy ones that taste like they're not—and these, doll, are exactly that.

—— TO THAT END /
THE ONLY RECIPES FOR ME
ARE THE EASY ONES THAT
TASTE LIKE THEY'RE NOT . . .

AND THESE, DOLL, ARE EXACTLY THAT.

PREVIOUS: Fresh cranberries make coupes of champagne even merrier at Dodson Epley's house.

OPPOSITE: Abraham Lincoln's favorite gingerbread recipe: still a winner, centuries later. To make, see the recipe on page 170.

In the dark days of winter, I gravitate to comfort foods, and that's what you'll find here. Buttery, creamy dreams that are high in calories but not in kitchen agony. Some of them were go-to recipes of boldfaced names, including Jackie Kennedy's Poulet a L'Estragon—a chicken dish as divine as her Givenchy dresses. Others are recipes I have been given or fallen in love with over the years and can't help but share here in hopes that you will fall in love with them, too.

I think a lot of people fall into the trap of making the same dishes year after year. That's wonderful if you actually like the meals and cookies in question. But if you don't, just skip Aunt Marilyn's pumpkin cheesecake and try something new. Life is far too short for ho-hum pastas and flavorless pies, and the Christmas season is even shorter.

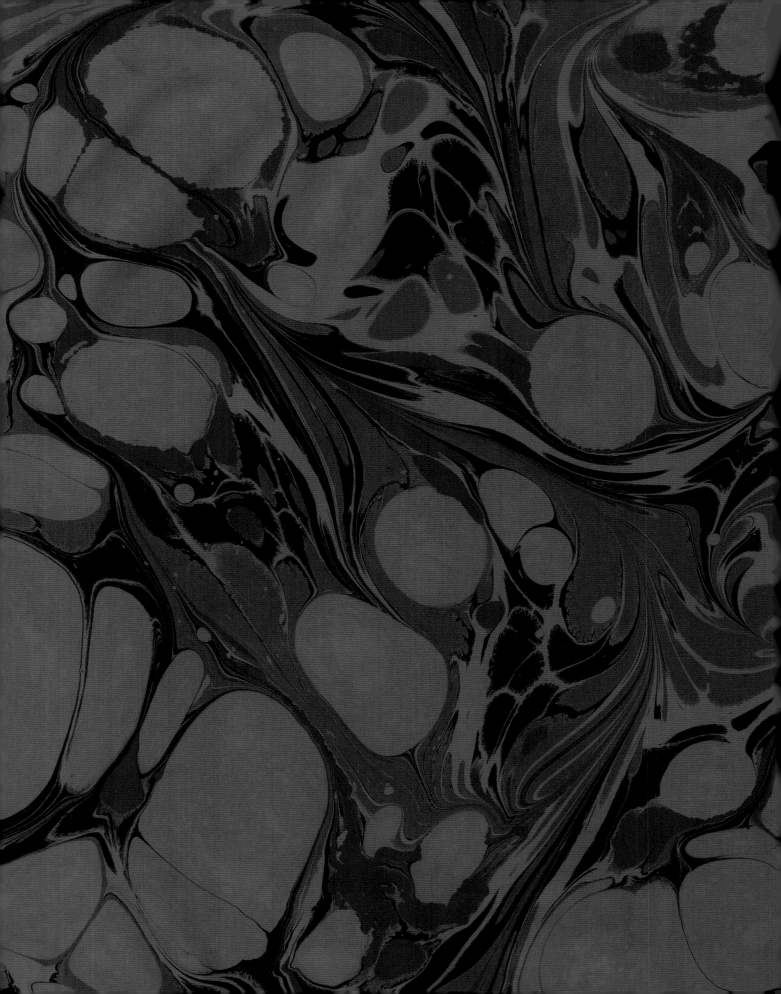

SAVORY

A VERY MERRY FOCACCIA

What the focaccia are you waiting for, honestly? This is arguably the most beautiful method of carb disbursement of the holiday season—and impossible to mess up. After you make your dough—allowing it to rest for 48 hours in the fridge for an airy texture—adorn its surface with a Christmas tree made of rosemary and sage leaves, cherry tomato ornaments, and red onion "tree stand" before baking. Fa-la-la!

MAKES 1 LARGE SLAB OF FOCACCIA

- 4 cups all-purpose flour
- 2 teaspoons kosher salt
- 2 teaspoons instant yeast
- 2 cups lukewarm water
- 1 teaspoon honey
- 3 tablespoons olive oil, divided
- 4 teaspoons whole rosemary leaves
- 4 teaspoons whole sage leaves
- 8 cherry tomatoes (yellow and red)
- ½ red onion, sliced to retain root
- Flaky Maldon sea salt

In a large bowl, stir together the flour, salt, and instant yeast. Add the water and honey and mix until you have dough. Coat the surface with 1 tablespoon olive oil and create an air-tight cover with plastic wrap. Place in your fridge for 48 hours.

Line a 9 x 13-inch pan with parchment paper, and pour 2 tablespoons olive oil into the center. Pull the dough out of the bowl and form it into a ball, then roll it in the pan, coating it in olive oil. Let the dough ball rest in the pan on your counter for 4 hours. Place an oven rack in the middle of your oven and preheat to 425°F. Coat your hands with olive oil and stretch the dough so that it covers the interior of the pan, pushing deep dimples into the dough surface with your fingers.

Adorn the surface of your dough with the rosemary, sage, tomato ornaments, and red onion tree stand to form a decorated tree. Sprinkle with sea salt. Bake for 25 to 30 minutes, until focaccia base becomes a crispy gold. Remove the pan from the oven and transfer the bread carefully to a cooling rack. Wait 10 minutes and enjoy.

PIMENTO CHEESE DIP

Every time I am south of the Mason-Dixon Line—which is often—I eat at least a cup of pimento cheese a day. This can't be helped; something about being in the humidity demands it. I discovered on our recent trip to North Carolina that the best pimento cheese dip is actually made with a sharper white cheddar rather than the traditional orange. With plenty of red pimentos and green jalapeños, you have yourself a traditional Christmas dip. I serve it with dry, crunchy sourdough flatbread crackers to balance the fatty heft of the mayo.

MAKES 8 SERVINGS

- 2 cups freshly grated extra-sharp white cheddar cheese
- 8 ounces cream cheese, softened
- ½ cup full-fat mayonnaise
- 2 medium-size jalapeños, seeds removed, minced
- 2 (4-ounce) jars pimento peppers, drained and minced
- ¼ teaspoon garlic salt (Lawry's preferred)
- ¼ teaspoon ground cayenne pepper
- ¼ teaspoon onion powder
- Kosher salt and ground black pepper

Gather ingredients—cheeses, mayonnaise, jalapeños, pimentos, garlic salt, cayenne pepper, and onion powder—into a bowl and mix. Season with salt and pepper to taste. Voilà!

JACKIE KENNEDY'S POULET A L'ESTRAGON

Tarragon is the herb I would take with me to the proverbial desert island. There's something about it that instantly transports me from suburbia to Provence, where I'm catching some sun on a café terrace along the Rhône. It doesn't surprise me that Mrs. Jackie Kennedy approved of this recipe. She submitted it for inclusion in *The First Ladies Cook Book*, which I've adapted here. It is exactly as creamy and dreamy as it sounds.

SERVES 4

- 2 tablespoons all-purpose flour
- Salt, to taste
- Ground black pepper, to taste
- 4 chicken legs
- 2 tablespoons clarified butter for sautéing
- 3 shallots—half sliced into rings, half finely chopped
- ½ cup dry white wine from France, such as a sauvignon blanc
- ½ cup chicken stock
- 1 bay leaf
- 1 pinch fresh thyme
- 2 stems fresh parsley
- 1 small bunch fresh tarragon, stems and leaves divided

SAUCE

- 1 cup heavy cream
- ½ cup Parmesan cheese, freshly grated

In a small bowl, combine the flour, salt, and black pepper. Coat the chicken legs with the flour mixture; reserving any flour mixture that is leftover. Melt the clarified butter in a pan over medium-high heat, then brown the chicken legs on all sides, about 2 minutes per side. Spread the shallots over chicken. Simmer for about 3 minutes. Add the wine, stock, and herbs, using only the tarragon stems; reserve the tarragon leaves. Cover and simmer the chicken for 25 minutes or until tender. When the chicken reaches an internal temperature of 165°F, remove the chicken from the pan and place it in a serving dish, covering it to keep it warm. Discard the bay leaf.

To prepare the sauce, add the cream, Parmesan, and any flour not used in coating chicken to the remaining drippings in the chicken pan. Simmer gently for a minute or two, until the sauce thickens. Pour the sauce over the chicken. Garnish with a flurry of tarragon leaves—some whole, some chopped.

ARTISANAL HERB BREAD

If you've ever wondered how to easily get perfect crispy-crusty bakery bread at home, this no-knead recipe originally adapted from Sullivan Street Bakery is it. The key is a Dutch oven or a heavy cast-iron pot with a lid to trap steam. If the surface is imperfect, I have good news: it will taste just as delicious as the Instagrammable one. Use rice flour to dust the top; it's less likely to scorch, so it highlights surface decorations in a snow white.

MAKES 1 LOAF

- 3¼ cups all-purpose flour
- 2 teaspoons fine sea salt
- 1 teaspoon honey
- ½ teaspoon active dry yeast
- 1½ cups warm water
- 1 tablespoon chopped fresh rosemary
- 1 tablespoon chopped fresh basil
- 4 garlic cloves, thinly sliced
- 1 tablespoon cornmeal
- ¼ cup rice flour

Stir together the flour, salt, honey, and yeast in a large bowl. Add warm water and stir with a wooden spoon until mixed. A "shaggy" look is to be expected, fret not. Cover the bowl with plastic wrap and let rise at room temperature for 12 hours. Pull the dough loose from the bowl and place onto a well-floured surface. Add the rosemary, basil, and garlic to the dough, then shape it into a round ball, folding it into itself until it begins to hold its shape. (You may need to add more flour if it's too sticky.) Set the dough ball on parchment paper and cover it with plastic wrap. Allow the dough to rise for 30 minutes as you preheat the oven, tightening the dough ball if it loses its shape. While the dough rises, place the Dutch oven (with lid on) in the center of the oven, then preheat the oven to 450°F.

Working on a flat surface, spread the cornmeal in a loaf-size circle on a piece of parchment paper. Place the dough on the cornmeal, and dust the top of the dough ball with the rice flour. Score the dough into the branched shape of an evergreen tree, and remove a bit of dough below the tree branches. Carefully place the dough—still on the parchment—inside the Dutch oven. Replace the lid, tucking all the parchment inside so it doesn't burn. Bake for 30 minutes. Remove the lid and bake for another 10 to 20 minutes, until the bread's surface is a tawny golden brown. Remove the pot from the oven and, using the parchment, gingerly transfer the bread to a wire cooling rack. Cool for 30 minutes before serving . . . if you can wait that long.

CHRISTMAS IN PUGLIA PASTA

"What? Another cream dish?" Yes, honey. Yes. It's sweater weather! This one is adapted from a recipe my best friend, Rachel, hooked me on, and it is almost guaranteed to make you feel like you're spending Christmas in southern Italy, even if you're actually in Des Moines. I promise. Serve with the crustiest, flakiest bread you can find. (Perhaps Artisanal Herb Bread, opposite.)

SERVES 4

- 2 tablespoons unsalted butter
- 4 garlic cloves, minced
- ½ teaspoon salt
- ½ teaspoon dried oregano
- ½ teaspoon crushed red pepper flakes
- ¼ teaspoon ground black pepper
- ¾ cup oil-packed sun-dried tomatoes, chopped
- 1 cup chicken broth
- 2 (15-ounce) cans cannellini beans, drained
- 1 pound orecchiette pasta
- 1 cup heavy cream
- 1 cup freshly grated Parmesan cheese; reserve ¼ cup for sprinkling
- 3 tablespoons chopped fresh basil, stems removed; divided
- 4 grilled chicken breasts (1 per serving), sliced into strips and kept warm

In a large pan over medium heat, melt the butter with the garlic, salt, oregano, crushed red pepper flakes, and ground black pepper. Cook for 2 minutes, until your kitchen smells utterly fabulous. Stir in the tomatoes, chicken broth, and cannellini beans, and simmer uncovered for 5 minutes.

While the sauce is simmering, cook the orecchiette pasta according to the package instructions and drain.

Remove the sauce from heat, stir in cream, ¾ cup Parmesan, and 2 tablespoons basil.

For each serving, plate the orecchiette pasta, top with a couple scoops of the sauce, sliced chicken, and sprinkles of Parmesan cheese and basil to taste.

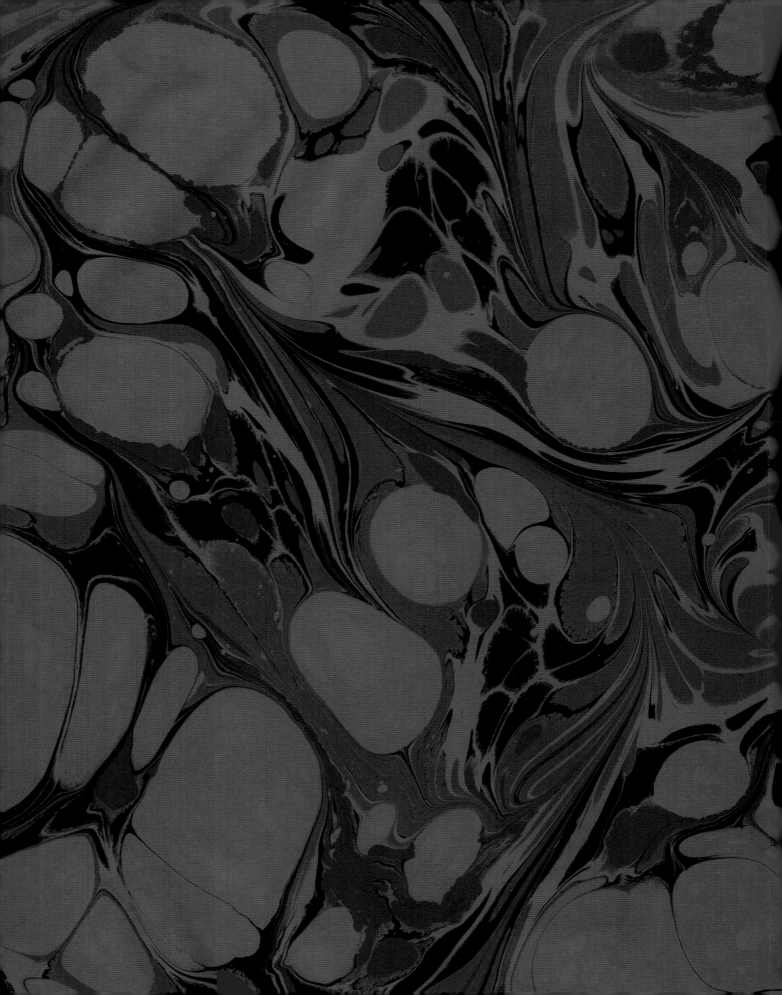

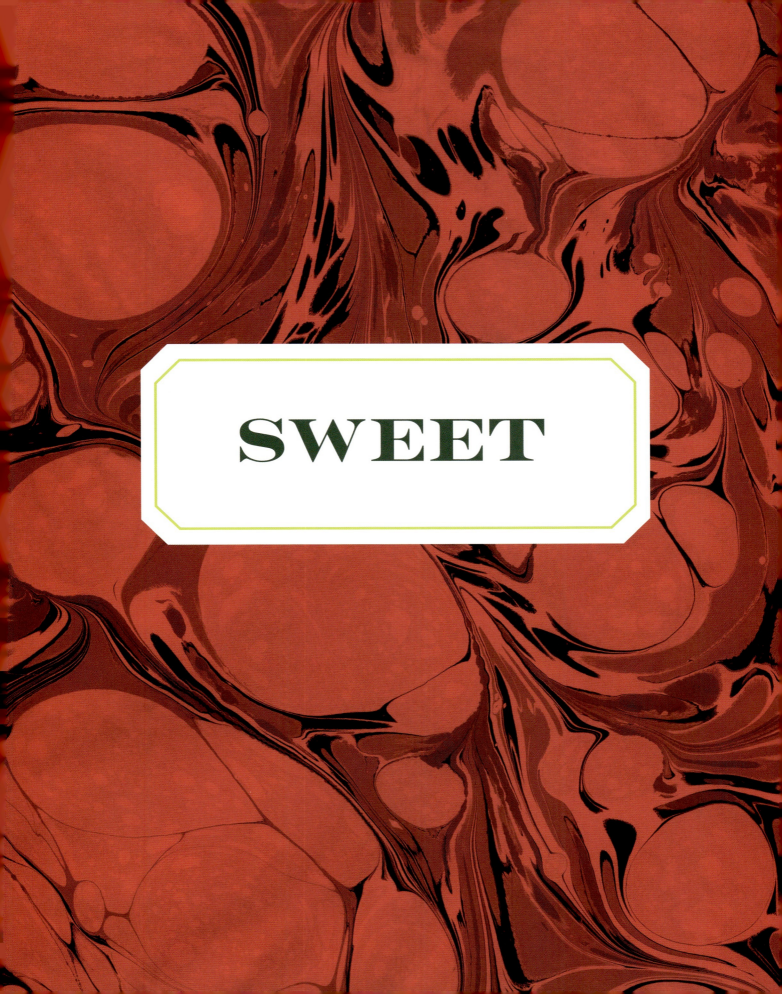

AMERICA'S BEST APPLE PIE RECIPE. REALLY.

I can't recall how I happened upon Nancie McDermott's cookbook *Southern Pies: A Gracious Plenty of Pie Recipes, From Lemon Chess to Chocolate Pecan*. But it is so fabulous that I quickly followed Nancie on Instagram, and soon we became Insta-friends. Her apple pie recipe is gooey and phenomenal—the kind of pie you can imagine tucking into at a roadside stand on that first crisp, sunny day of autumn. Speaking of gracious, Nancie allowed me to share her apple pie recipe, which I've adapted slightly—to have a traditional single layer rather than two—here. You won't find one better.

MAKES ONE 9-INCH PIE

PIE CRUST

- 2 cups all-purpose flour
- 1 teaspoon salt
- ½ cup very cold unsalted butter, cut into ½-inch cubes
- 4 to 6 tablespoons ice water
- 1 teaspoon white vinegar

FILLING

- 2¼ pounds cooking apples, such as Granny Smith, Rome Beauty, or Empire
- 1½ cups granulated sugar
- 1½ teaspoons ground cinnamon
- 1 teaspoon ground nutmeg
- ⅓ cup salted butter
- ¼ cup water
- 2 tablespoons all-purpose flour

In the work bowl of a food processor fitted with a metal blade, combine the flour and salt, and pulse for 10 seconds. Add the butter and pulse until mixture resembles coarse sand with some small lumps, about 40 seconds. Add 3 tablespoons ice water and the vinegar and pulse up to 7 times, until the dough barely holds together. Add another tablespoon or two of ice water to bring the ingredients together, if needed. Turn the dough onto a sheet of plastic wrap, create 2 separate disks of equal size—one for the bottom pie crust, and one for a decorative top layer—and refrigerate

continued

them for at least 1 hour. Set them out at room temperature for 10 minutes before rolling. Roll out one disk on a lightly floured surface until it's about 10 inches in diameter and ⅛-inch thick, and transfer it into a 9-inch pie plate as the bottom pie crust. Press the dough gently into the plate, trim any excess dough, and place the pie plate in the fridge. (I save the excess dough and second disk to decoratively top my apple pie with.)

Preheat the oven to 375°F.

Peel and core the apples, then cut into ½-inch-thick slices. (You'll have about 5 cups.) In a large saucepan, combine the apples, sugar, cinnamon, and nutmeg, and toss to combine evenly and well. Add the butter and water, bringing to a gentle boil over medium-high heat. Reduce the heat to maintain a gentle simmer and cook until the apples are tender when poked with a fork, 20 to 30 minutes. Stir in the flour and cook 10 minutes more, stirring now and then.

Remove the bottom pie crust from the fridge and fill with the apple mixture. Roll out the remaining pie crust to use to top the pie. (I like to use cookie cutters to create decorative crust pieces that I adorn the top of the pie with—stars, trees, monograms, you name it—sticking it together with an egg wash and using an egg wash across the entire pie crust to prevent burning.) Place the pie on the center rack of the oven and bake until the pastry is golden brown and the apple filling is bubbling, 20 to 25 minutes. Place the pie on a cooling rack for 15 minutes. Serve warm or at room temperature, preferably with a side of vanilla ice cream.

VERY, VERY ADDICTIVE CHERRY BARS

My great-grandmother (and my namesake, Kathryn) made these cherry bars every Christmas in the brutal Midwest winters. Her legions of progeny now follow suit, although most of us live in warmer climes. I've adapted the recipe—originally given to her by her friend Bizz (although I think it may have come from a Betty Crocker cookbook)—to include Luxardo cherries, but if you stick to standard maraschino for brighter color, I won't tell. They have a bit more zing. Don't be put off by the coconut. You can't really taste it; it's more of a backup dancer than the star of the show. Holly jolly!

MAKES 12 BARS

½ cup salted butter (I prefer Kerrygold), softened, plus more for greasing the pan

1¼ cups all-purpose flour, divided

3 tablespoons powdered sugar

2 eggs

1 cup granulated sugar

¾ cup chopped pecans

½ cup sweetened flaked coconut

½ cup chopped Luxardo cherries, drained

½ teaspoon baking powder

¼ teaspoon salt

1 teaspoon pure vanilla extract

Heat the oven to 350°F. Grease an 8-inch square pan with butter. In a medium bowl, mix 1 cup flour, the butter, and the powdered sugar with a spoon until the flour is moistened. Using the back of a spoon, press the mixture into the prepared pan. Bake for 10 minutes, then remove from the oven to cool completely.

In a large bowl, beat the eggs, then stir in the sugar, pecans, coconut, cherries, the remaining ¼ cup flour, baking powder, salt, and vanilla. Pour the mixture into the pan over the prepared crust. Return the pan to the oven and bake for 25 to 30 minutes, or until the surface is golden brown. Remove from the oven and allow to cool completely, around 30 minutes. Cut into bars for serving.

MOLLY'S SHORTBREAD

Molly, my darling nonagenarian neighbor in New York City, taught me some important lessons during our years of sharing a wall: (1) age is just a number, (2) invite a stranger in for a drink and you may just meet your next bestie, (3) how to make the best shortbread you've ever had in your life. (Molly immigrated from Scotland as a child. She delivered tins of this recipe to friends and family every year—our tin only lasted about a day.)

Molly always said that one key to the perfect shortbread is to seek out the very fine sugar that bartenders use to rim glasses. Another is to treat it like dough. "You knead it!" Molly would say, with a flourish of her fingers. A glass of scotch as accompaniment is ideal but not required.

MAKES 2 POUNDS

- 1 pound salted butter, room temperature
- 1 cup superfine sugar, plus another tablespoon for sprinkling
- 5 cups flour

Preheat the oven to 300°F, and line cookie tins with waxed paper. Knead the butter and sugar together until well combined. Add the flour, a small amount at a time until the mixture looks like sand. Place the dough into a 10 x 15-inch jelly-roll pan. (I like those from Nordic Ware, made in the US.) Prick the surface with the tines of a fork, then bake for 1 hour. Sprinkle it with sugar and cut into squares. Cool, then place the shortbread in the prepared cookie tins. Await adoration.

CROISSANTS FIT FOR A QUEEN

Croissants don't need to be fancified. Or do they? It's nice to do one special-feeling thing when you host—something that your guests will remember but that you can easily do without losing your mind. When you're hosting a Christmastime breakfast, this is it: croissants dipped in chocolate and adorned with whatever strikes your fancy, be it candied citrus, gold leaf, or a studding of slivered almonds and pine nuts.

MAKES 6 CROISSANTS

12 ounces milk chocolate chips

1 teaspoon coconut oil

6 fresh croissants (purchased from your local boulangerie or bakery the day of your event—always; despite what some people will tell you, quality croissants do not last!)

OPTIONAL

Slivered almonds

Pine nuts

Coarse salt

Gold leaf

Candied citrus

Combine the milk chocolate chips and coconut oil, for shine, in a large bowl and microwave for 30 seconds. Stir. Microwave for 30 seconds. Stir. And so on, until the chocolate has transformed into a melted miracle. (I know—actual chefs prefer a double boiler. But I'm tired and this works. I honestly can't taste the difference.)

Dip the croissants into the chocolate and decorate however you wish. Here, I used slivered almonds, pine nuts, and a snowflake-like dusting of coarse salt.

CHRISTMAS CONFETTI CHOCOLATE BARK

This Christmas Confetti Chocolate Bark is everything I love in a foodstuff: easy to make and highly glamorous.

MAKES ABOUT 8 PIECES

12 ounces dark or milk chocolate chips

1 tablespoon coconut oil

1 tablespoon granulated sugar

OPTIONAL

7 dried orange slices

1 cup dried strawberry slices (often available in the toddler food section)

1 cup potato chips of your choice (I prefer classic or crinkle cut)

1 cup pretzel sticks

½ teaspoon coarse sea salt

2 sheets edible gold leaf

Place the chocolate, oil, and sugar into a bowl and microwave in 30-second bursts, stirring in between, until the chocolate is melted. Spoon the melted chocolate onto a parchment-topped baking sheet and spread into a slab about ¼-inch thick. Top with your Christmas confetti of choice. (Here, I pressed in the dried orange slices first, then the strawberries, then added everything else around them. Gold—notoriously difficult to work with—goes last.) Place the baking sheet in the freezer for 10 minutes, until the chocolate is hardened, then cut and serve however you like.

CRAN-ORANGE BISCOTTI

This season, it helps to have a little something sweet—but not saccharine—to accompany that first cuppa.

MAKES 12 BISCOTTI

- ½ cup salted butter (I like Kerrygold), room temperature
- 1 cup granulated sugar
- 2 eggs
- 1 tablespoon finely grated orange zest
- 2 teaspoons orange juice
- 2 ¾ cups all-purpose flour
- 1 teaspoon baking powder
- ½ teaspoon baking soda
- ½ teaspoon sea salt
- ¾ cup sweetened dried cranberries

FROSTING AND TOPPINGS

- 1 package white chocolate chips (about 1 ½ cups)
- 1 teaspoon coconut oil
- 2 tablespoons finely grated orange zest
- Sea salt

Preheat oven to 350°F and line a baking sheet with parchment paper. In a large bowl, mix the butter and sugar until creamy, then add the eggs, orange zest, and orange juice. In a separate bowl, combine the flour, baking powder, baking soda, and salt. Add the dry ingredients to wet ingredients, mixing until you have a dough, then stir in the dried cranberries. Shape the dough into 2 logs about three inches wide and one inch tall, and bake on the prepared baking sheet until brown and a fork inserted into each log comes out clean, 23 to 33 minutes. Set the baking sheet on a wire rack to cool. Using your sharpest knife, slice the logs diagonally, then lay each cut slice on your now cooled and still parchment-topped baking sheet. Bake again, about 15 minutes, until the biscotti are crisp. Remove biscotti from the baking sheet and allow them to cool on wire racks.

In a clean bowl, heat the white chocolate chips and coconut oil in the microwave in 30-second bursts, stirring in between, until you have a smooth melted chocolate. Dip one side of each of the cooled biscotti, place on a fresh sheet of parchment, and sprinkle with orange zest and sea salt to taste. Allow to dry.

ABRAHAM LINCOLN'S GINGERBREAD

President Lincoln loved gingerbread cookies. He once famously told a story from his childhood about eating some under a tree and giving one to a down-on-his-luck neighbor boy. When the new friend asked for another, Lincoln recalls the boy saying, "Abe, I don't suppose anybody on earth likes gingerbread better than I do—and gets less of it."

This recipe was shared by Mary Todd Lincoln in Sarah Hale's 1841 publication *The Good Housekeeper*. Although the couple was then estranged (after breaking off their engagement), I think we can assume that President Lincoln later enjoyed the recipe when the duo was married and ensconced in the White House—and that he shared his cookies freely.

Take 1½ pounds flour and rub it into ½ pound butter, add ½ pound brown sugar and a ½ pint of molasses, 2 tablespoons cream, 1 teaspoon pearlash [potassium carbonate], and ginger to the taste. Make it into a stiff paste, and roll it out thin. Put it on buttered tins, and bake in moderate oven.

TWENTY-FIRST-CENTURY UPDATE

MAKES 24 COOKIES

- 5½ cups flour
- 2 cups salted butter, room temperature
- 1⅛ cups brown sugar
- 1¼ cups molasses
- 2 tablespoons heavy cream
- ½ teaspoon baking soda
- 1 tablespoon ground ginger

Preheat the oven to 350°F and line a baking sheet with parchment paper. Rub the flour into the butter. Add the brown sugar, molasses, cream, baking soda, and ginger. Work the dough into a stiff paste, then wrap it tightly in plastic wrap and put in the fridge for 2 hours (or overnight) before rolling thin to cut into shapes with your favorite cookie cutters. Place the cookies on the prepared baking sheet and bake for 10 to 12 minutes.

While Lincoln's recipe doesn't call for decorating, I'm quite sure that would have been approved by presidential order!

CASS'S CHEESECAKE

I once interviewed the lovely Ina Garten at her home in East Hampton, where she was working on her forty-fifth version of a scone recipe. And still, after all that tinkering, the scones weren't quite right—so into the bin they went. My late mother-in-law, Cass (RIP, queen!), was like that . . . always toiling to get a recipe perfect. She made the best cheesecake in the world—In. The. *World*. She was incredibly generous and would be delighted that I've shared her recipe here. The problem is, it's too good; you'll want to eat nothing else, and it will show. You've been warned! Also, puhleeze don't use off-brand grahams. The extra 50 cents is worth it for Honey Maid.

MAKES ONE 8-INCH CAKE

CRUST

- 1½ cups (about 2 sleeves) graham crackers (preferably Honey Maid), whirred into crumbs
- ¼ cup granulated sugar
- 1 teaspoon ground cinnamon
- ¼ teaspoon ground nutmeg
- ½ teaspoon ground cloves
- ⅓ cup salted butter, melted

FILLING

- 2 eggs
- ½ cup granulated sugar
- 2 (8-ounce) packages cream cheese, softened
- 2 teaspoons pure vanilla extract

SOUR CREAM TOPPING

- 1 pint sour cream
- 6 tablespoons granulated sugar
- 2 teaspoons pure vanilla extract

Preheat the oven to 350°F. Butter an 8-inch springform pan.

To make the crust, combine the graham cracker crumbs, sugar, cinnamon, nutmeg, cloves, and melted butter in a medium-sized mixing bowl. To form cheesecake crust, press the mixture into the prepared pan, working it into a thick slab base with side walls an inch or two up the sides of the pan. (You can use a measuring cup to help press it in.) Bake the crust for 5 minutes.

Increase the oven temperature to 375°F. To make the cheesecake filling, beat the eggs until light, add ½ cup sugar, and beat for 5 more minutes. Add the cream cheese and vanilla and mix well. Pour the filling into the prepared crust and bake for 20 minutes. Cool the cheesecake for 15 minutes.

Increase the oven temperature to 475°F. Combine the sour cream, sugar, and vanilla and blend well. Pour the topping over the filling and bake for 5 minutes. Cool the cheesecake on the counter, then tuck it in the fridge and let it rest overnight before indulging.

AUDREY HEPBURN'S CHOCOLATE CAKE

Audrey Hepburn adored chocolate—it was reportedly the first thing she ate after Holland was liberated from World War II, when a soldier handed her a chocolate bar. This recipe is adapted from her son Luca Dotti's book *Audrey at Home*—and is absolutely as life-affirming as she would have wanted.

MAKES 1 (10-INCH) CAKE

8 tablespoons (1 stick) unsalted butter, cut into small pieces, plus extra for greasing

Flour for dusting the pan

11 ounces unsweetened high-quality dark chocolate, chopped

¼ cup whole milk

8 eggs, separated

1 cup granulated sugar

Powdered sugar

Whipped cream or vanilla ice cream

Preheat the oven to 400°F. Butter and flour a 10- or 12-inch round baking pan. Melt the chocolate with the milk in a *bain-marie* (a very Audrey term for a double boiler). Add the butter and stir to blend thoroughly. Turn off the heat and mix in 8 egg yolks.

In a separate bowl, gradually add the sugar to the egg whites and whip to form stiff peaks. Gently fold into the chocolate–egg yolk mixture. Pour into the prepared pan.

Bake in the preheated oven for 30 minutes. Turn off the oven, open the door, and leave the cake inside for a few minutes. This will prevent the crust from cracking.

Remove from the oven and cool for about 10 minutes before removing from the pan and turning it over onto a cake plate. Sprinkle with powdered sugar and serve with whipped cream or ice cream.

ORANGE COOKIES

In the frigid depths of winter, a bit of citrusy zing on the palette is a joy. For centuries, oranges were only enjoyed by those deeply pocketed enough to have an orangery—or pay the then-exorbitant cost for the fruit. While an orange at the toe of a Christmas stocking is a throwback to the bags of gold left by Saint Nicholas, these days many of us would prefer these frosted orange cookies.

MAKES 2 DOZEN COOKIES

- 1 cup salted butter (I prefer Kerrygold)
- 1½ cups granulated sugar
- 1 cup sour cream
- 2 eggs
- 3 tablespoons finely grated orange zest
- 4 cups all-purpose flour
- 1 teaspoon baking powder
- 1 teaspoon baking soda
- ½ teaspoon salt
- ⅔ cup freshly squeezed orange juice

ICING

- ¼ cup salted butter, melted
- 2 cups powdered sugar
- 1 tablespoon finely grated orange zest
- 3 tablespoons freshly squeezed orange juice
- 10 dried orange slices (available at health food stores), sliced into narrow slivers

Preheat the oven to 375°F, and line a baking sheet with parchment paper.

In a medium bowl, cream together the butter, sugar, and sour cream until smooth and lump-free. Beat in the eggs one at a time, then stir in the orange zest.

In a separate bowl, combine the flour with the baking powder, baking soda, and salt. Gradually combine the dry ingredients into the creamed mixture alternately with the orange juice. Drop the cookie dough by teaspoonfuls onto the prepared baking sheet. Bake for 8 to 10 minutes. Allow the cookies to cool for 2 minutes on the baking sheet so they develop a slightly crisp base, then transfer the cookies to a wire rack to cool completely.

In a large bowl, stir together the melted butter, powdered sugar, and orange zest. Mix in the orange juice, 1 tablespoon at a time, until you've achieved a thick frosting consistency. When the cookies have fully cooled, use a fork to spread the frosting over the top of each cookie, then top with slivers of dried oranges.

DINNER PARTY PLAYLIST

◆

You don't want the overwhelming scent of flowers at a dinner party, and you don't want overwhelming music, either. Turn these tracks on low and slow to keep conversation going.

"2,000 Miles"–The Pretenders

"Winter Wonderland"–Ella Fitzgerald

"The Bells of Dublin"–The Chieftains

"Dance of the Sugar Plum Fairy"–Tchaikovsky

"Little Drummer Boy"–David Bowie and Bing Crosby

"Winter Wonderland"–The Wynton Marsalis Quintet

"Oh Come Emmanuel"–Aliqua

"We're Goin' To the Country"–Sufjan Stevens

"Merry Christmas, Baby"–Charles Brown

"O Tannenbaum"–Vince Guaraldi Trio

You Eat Like a Queen. Really, You Do.

Every once in a while I cry over spilled milk (or malbec) and have to remind myself: I have it better than like 99.79 percent of my ancestors. Not very many generations ago, the bounty of the Christmas table would not have been bountiful at all, at least for my wan people of the British Isles, who might have counted themselves lucky to have a boiled potato or porridge in the offing. At that time, only a very, very few people in the history of humanity had tasted a pineapple, much less a Ladurée macaron or Ossetra caviar! While that's just as true today in so many places in this world, it's easy to take for granted. Especially when you're used to grocery stores stocked to the rafters and, as I have, curated local produce delivered to your door.

So if my turkey emerges a whisper too dry or my gravy lands lumpy and ho-hum on the palate, I don't give it a second thought. It just doesn't matter. We're together, we're healthy, and we're soon to be fed. Jimmy was right—it's a wonderful life.

PREVIOUS: Ruby red glassware sets Francis' holiday table aglow.

OPPOSITE: Parkey and his family host an annual champagne-and-French fry pre-party to gear up for a yearly fête nearby, where a full dinner is served. What could be more fun?

Champagne flutes were popularized in the Art Deco era, when their tall, narrow shapes were prized for keeping bubbles bubbly into the wee hours. They're even more festive served on a silver tray, as Parkey has here.

06/

HANDMADE BUT HAUTE
DIY GIFTS

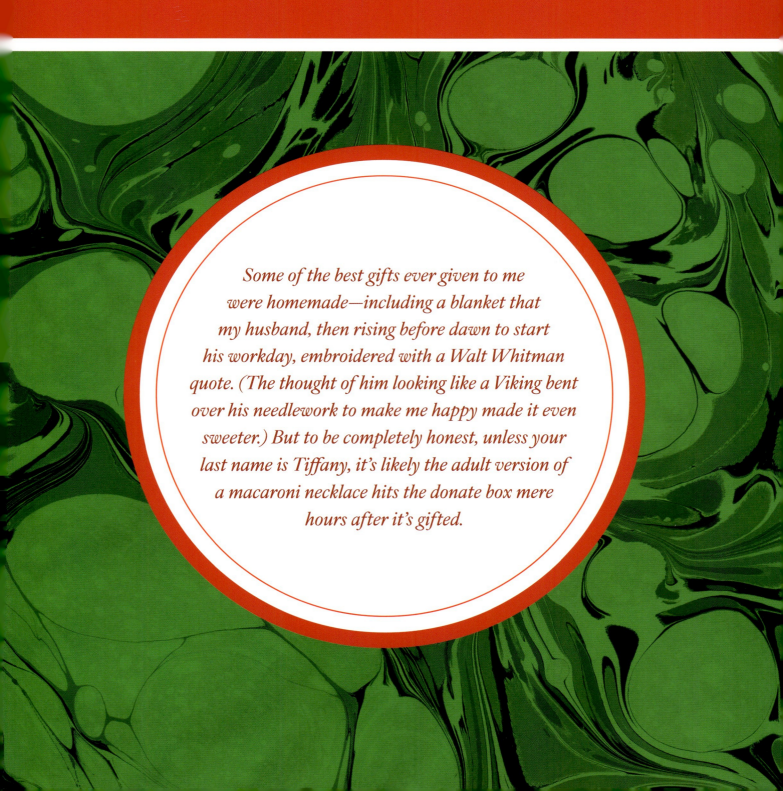

Some of the best gifts ever given to me were homemade—including a blanket that my husband, then rising before dawn to start his workday, embroidered with a Walt Whitman quote. (The thought of him looking like a Viking bent over his needlework to make me happy made it even sweeter.) But to be completely honest, unless your last name is Tiffany, it's likely the adult version of a macaroni necklace hits the donate box mere hours after it's gifted.

——— I LIKE TO COME UP WITH DIY GIFTS THAT ARE EDIBLE OR OTHERWISE IMPERMANENT SO THAT **THEY'RE MORE LIKELY TO BE ENJOYED.**

MELT & POUR SOAP

Pretty as a frozen pond, clear glycerin soaps are gemlike bathing beauties. They can be tailored to the season with scent (peppermint or orange-cinnamon, for example) and even trinkets suspended within, such as cinnamon sticks and dried orange slices or a miniature deer that emerges from the bar over time.

MAKES ABOUT 10 LARGE (OR 20 SMALL) SOAP BARS

MATERIALS (AVAILABLE AT CRAFT SHOPS)

- Glycerin soap base
- Isopropyl alcohol in a spray bottle (to eliminate bubbles)
- Essential oils (optional; stick with something near-universally liked, such as mint or lavender)

OPTIONAL ADD-INS

- Soap colorants
- Dried herbs or flowers
- Earth-friendly glitter
- Plastic toy deer

EQUIPMENT

- Microwave-safe container
- Silicone spoon for stirring
- Silicone soap molds (Etsy for custom-made)

Cut the glycerin soap base into small chunks for easier melting and place in a microwave-safe bowl. Microwave in 30-second intervals, stirring between each burst until melted. Stir in any of your chosen essential oils and colorants. Place dried herbs or flowers, glitter, and/or toy deer into your soap molds, then pour in the melted soap. Lightly spritz the surface of the soap with the alcohol to eradicate any air bubbles. Allow soap to set overnight, then remove from molds. Package prettily.

BATH BOMBS

Tweenagers have it right: these will never get old. To make yours specific to the Christmas season, consider whipping up "snowballs" by mixing in shimmering biodegradable glitter and a holiday-worthy essential oil duo, such as vanilla and peppermint.

MAKES 3 BATH BOMBS

DRY INGREDIENTS

1 cup baking soda

½ cup citric acid, for fizz

½ cup Epsom salt

½ cup cornstarch

WET INGREDIENTS

2½ tablespoons coconut oil

¾ tablespoon water

1 teaspoon essential oil, such as vanilla and peppermint

1 to 2 drops food coloring

OPTIONAL ADD-INS

Dried flowers or herbs

Earth-friendly glitter

EQUIPMENT

Mixing bowls

Microwave-safe bowl

Whisk

Silicone bath-bomb molds

Measuring cups and spoons

Spray bottle filled with water

In a large bowl, combine the baking soda, citric acid, Epsom salt, and cornstarch, whisking until combined. In a separate large microwave-safe bowl, microwave the coconut oil in 30-second bursts until fully melted; add the water, essential oil, and food coloring, and stir until blended. Very gradually pour the melted coconut oil into the dry ingredients. It should look like wet sand and hold its shape. Too dry? Spray with a bit of water (but not too much—you don't want to set off the fizz). Tightly pack the sand-like mixture into bath-bomb molds, as if you're building a sandcastle at the beach. Gingerly place them on a piece of parchment paper to dry for 24 hours before wrapping and gifting.

ORANGE-CRANBERRY SAUCE

Yeah, it's a Thanksgiving classic. But it's also a de facto jam that's surprisingly good with *everrrrrything*—from a cheese plate to Greek yogurt—and a much-enjoyed gift in the holiday season, especially when charmingly wrapped.

MAKES 4 CUPS

- 3 cups fresh cranberries
- 1 cup granulated sugar, or more to taste
- ½ cup freshly squeezed orange juice
- Freshly zested peel of 1 orange
- ¼ cup water
- 1 pinch table salt

OPTIONAL

- ¼ teaspoon ground cinnamon
- ¼ teaspoon ground nutmeg
- ¼ teaspoon ground ginger
- A splash of Grand Marnier, for orange zing

Rinse the cranberries under cold water and place in a saucepan with the sugar, orange juice, orange zest, water, and salt, as well as the optional spices and liqueur, if you desire. Place the saucepan over medium heat and stir to help dissolve the sugar. Once the mixture starts to simmer, reduce the heat to low (the cranberries will begin to pop in the heat). Allow to cook until the sauce has thickened, about 15 minutes, mashing the cranberries with a potato masher and stirring occasionally. Taste and add more sugar, if necessary. Remove from heat and cool. Transfer to pantry jars—I like those with the leakproof, swing-top lids—and keep refrigerated, where it will last about 1 week (but probably will be eaten within 2 days).

FA-LA-LAVORED OLIVE OIL

The only thing better than freshly baked bread is freshly baked bread dripping with an infused olive oil. No one will balk at this gift—trust me—and it looks gorgeous on a countertop.

MAKES 34 OUNCES, OR 2 (17-OUNCE) DISPENSERS

2 (17-ounce) glass olive oil dispensers, sterilized

2 liters extra-virgin olive oil (Costco has a nice organic version in bulk)

Your choice of flavorings—peeled garlic cloves, rosemary (which looks like an evergreen tree branch), lemon . . . your options are endless, but be sure they're washed and dried

In a saucepan over low heat, warm the amount of olive oil you need to nearly fill a jar, without letting it boil. Remove from heat and add your flavorings of choice. Let it all steep together, stirring every few minutes. Allow to cool, pour into your olive oil dispenser, cap, and fancify with a bow. Encourage lucky recipients to indulge within a week.

EGGNOG RIMMING SPICE

Academics agree that eggnog likely derived from posset, a milky grog of medieval Britain that, frankly, doesn't sound very appetizing. Yet eggnog is our nightly addiction as soon as it hits the shelves. I drink the oat milk, nonalcoholic version on weeknights and am more likely go full-throttle with a Southern Comfort, full-cal, nip-of-whiskey tipple come Friday. But either way, I give myself a more special-feeling moment by rimming my glass with this mix of spices that, packaged in a teensy spice jar, is a welcome treat for friends this time of year.

MAKES ENOUGH TO RIM 6 DRINKS

- 4 tablespoons superfine sugar
- 2 tablespoons ground cinnamon
- 1 tablespoon ground nutmeg
- ½ teaspoon ground ginger

Mix all ingredients and keep in an air-tight container. To rim your glass with it, pour your rimming spice onto a plate, moisten the edge of your drinking glass with a lemon wedge, then dip into the rimming spice.

GIFT WRAPPING THAT
WOWS

◆

Christmas is for the kids … in all of us. While as a busy working mother I've certainly had my quick-ship and extremely belated moments (apologies, loved ones … my brain is like day-old granola!), I'm still a firm believer that gifts are best served properly—if not beautifully—wrapped. It pains me when packages from a certain megaretailer arrive as "gifts," swaddled only in a cardboard box and plasticky bags, a card printed cryptically, like a castaway receipt. When you take the five minutes required to adorn a gift, you've made not only the act of giving more special but also the receiver feel that much more cherished.

I know, I know—I'm piling on to the never-ending holiday to-do list! Don't worry, we'll make this fun. I have a few hacks to help kick off a happy, wrappy experience.

You need a gift-wrapping station. It doesn't need to be a full room, although power to those Marthas who have one! It does need to be a decently sized table with nothing on it. Corral everything you need in one accessible place, such as a bin on a storage shelf that always contains the following: quality gift wrap in solids and patterns, scissors (I'm a Fiskars floozy), plenty of "disappearing" tape, sumptuous ribbons (even children can appreciate the tactility and sheen of velvet), cards and gift tags, and pens. Bonus points if you have a topper for the bow of each gift—like an unbreakable ornament, a sprig of evergreen (even if it's faux), a lollipop for a child …

Prevent wrapping fatigue. Doing all your gift-wrapping in one all-nighter is insanity and a recipe for papercuts to boot. Do yourself a favor and wrap gifts as they come in, not in one unenchanted evening.

Wrap gifts with a show you love on in the background. I can accomplish almost any household task if I have something I don't need to (ahem) watch on in the background. Key example: an episode of *Frasier* is so delightfully droll that listening to it is all the entertainment I need. (See page 114 for a list of my basic faves.) Put your headphones in, hit play, and let the wrapping begin.

07/

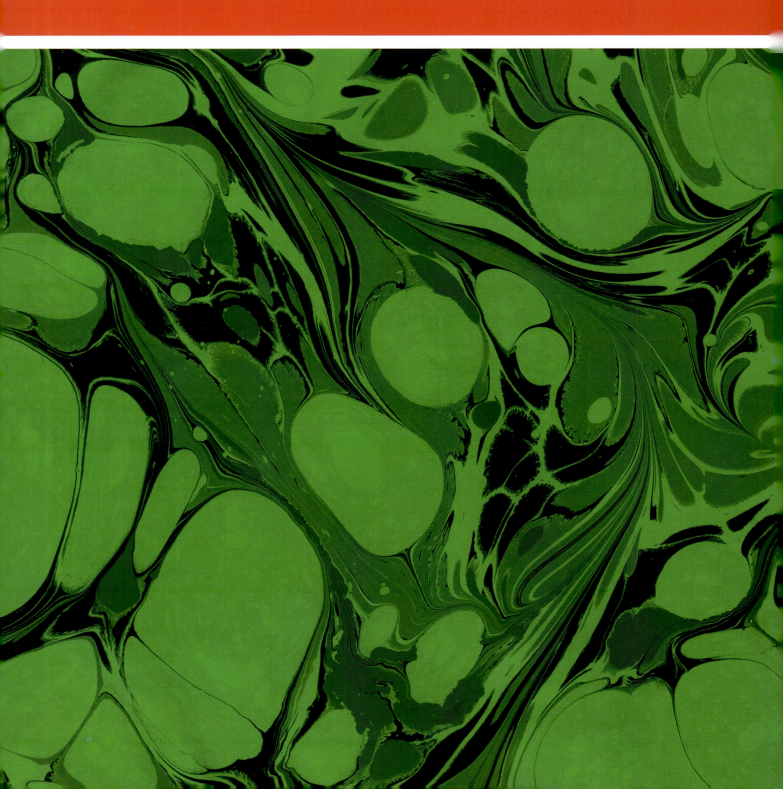

(SNOW) BOOT CAMP

In this chapter, you'll find a month-by-month, plan-ahead to-do list . . . because holiday sanity is a great gift to yourself (and everyone you live with).

— CHRISTMAS IS NOT A TIME OR A SEASON, BUT

A STATE OF MIND.

—CALVIN COOLIDGE

JANUARY

Indulge in R&R. 'Tis the season for much-deserved self-care. I book myself a post-holiday spa treatment every year, and I imagine Ms. Claus does the same. Highly recommended.

Take the tree down. And everything else. Decked-out halls feel special because they're rare ... ideally only enjoyed for a few months a year. It's like eggnog—they don't sell it in July for a reason!

Hit the sales. Now is the time to stock up on coveted decor, faux greenery, lights, and gift wrap, often at a steep discount.

Write your thank-yous. The 1920s doyenne of graciousness Emily Post was right: prompt thank-you notes are a must. Try to get them done in January, if possible, or you may forget entirely. (Guilty!)

FEBRUARY

Begin the gift list. Start brainstorming gift ideas for family and friends. (It's never too early, and it will keep a little elfin magic in your holiday step in the off season!) Don't forget the pets and anyone who assists you regularly (housekeepers, hairdressers), who will likely be delighted by the gesture.

Scour Facebook Marketplace. Generally, those who are getting rid of holiday baubles do so just after the season is over, and they may be willing to offload exquisite things for a song.

Begin DIY projects. Crafternoons are way more enjoyable when they're leisurely: nobody wants a hot-glue gun to their head! If you're going to attempt DIY bounty, begin early, tackling a craft a month until you're done.

MARCH

Update your address book. Ensure your Rolodex for holiday cards and invites is up to date. I, a Luddite, once buckled down and created an Excel spreadsheet that I could upload to print addresses with Avery labels. Now I can use it every year—printing all my labels essentially at the push of a button.

Plan holiday travel. The early bird gets the goooood Airbnb. If you plan to travel, now is the time to begin poking around and booking your stays and flights.

PREVIOUS: A bowl of mandarins (their leaves intact), manicured boxwoods, and a square wreath say "holiday" without a whiff of the cliché in Connor's office.

OPPOSITE: Enamel and silver Reed & Barton bowls in Francis' living room transform ornaments into a moment of visual candy.

APRIL

Take inventory. Make your list and check it thrice, ensuring you have stockpiled enough tape, ribbons, thank-you notes, and other musts for the season ahead.

MAY

Make design tweaks. Those things that are driving you batty in your home? The light fixture that never felt quite right, the too-low coffee table? Fix them now and you'll enjoy the space all the more when the holidays roll around.

Spring clean. Deep clean your home (or hire someone to do it for you) to get those less-regularly perfected things, like chandeliers and baseboards. This is also the time to do touch-up painting and scuff removal.

JUNE

Start stocking up. Keep an eye out for sales on things that will last in storage (or the deep freezer) until Christmas, such as canned pumpkin and sugar.

Book very merry activities. We love to do all the Christmassy things here in Colorado—the Polar Express train ride, the plays, the lights at the botanical garden. But I've found I need to book our tickets at the start of summer to ensure our spots. I bungled it one year and called Denver's grande dame for a Christmas Tea reservation in September, and he all but laughed in my face: "Those get booked by July." Never. Again.

JULY

Hit the Christmas-in-July sales. If you've got extra storage space, take advantage of mid-year sales. Prices on faux trees, especially, often get slashed this time of year.

Don't want to mar the exquisite woodwork on your mantel? Do as Francis has done in his 1910 New York City abode and hang your stockings from your fireplace tool stand.

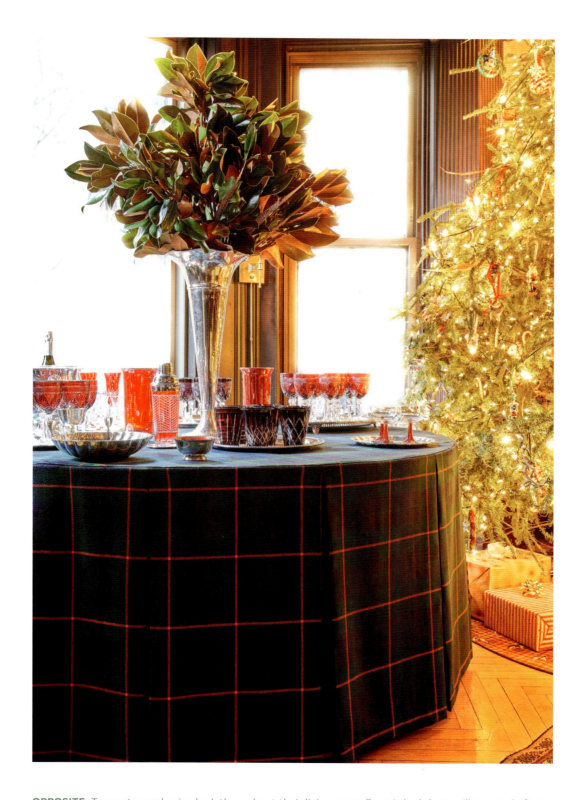

OPPOSITE: To create a cohesive look throughout their living room, Francis had throw pillows made from the same tartan he chose for his table skirt.

ABOVE: The custom tartan Francis selected for his table skirt appears all the more tailored with box pleats.

AUGUST

Plan for incoming guests. That old adage about houseguests, like fish, starting to stink after three days is less true when you pamper them. Put together a few indulgent activities, meals, and treats. (Bedside flowers and a snack basket will help them feel cherished.)

SEPTEMBER

Plan your holiday cards. Start designing or crafting your holiday cards when that first whiff of autumn hits the air. I once was so late that I had to send out Valentines! Learn from my mistakes and get them done by the end of September. Order your stamps, too; you can find a great selection of seasonal stamps at the USPS Postal Store website.

Review recipes. If pumpkin spice lattes are for sale anywhere, it's not too early to test potential Christmas recipes.

Check your gift lists. I keep these on my phone so no one will find them and know what I'm planning. I try to get all gift shopping (and even wrapping) done by Halloween, so I can truly relax and enjoy the season.

OCTOBER

Pull together your Christmas outfits. It might sound silly, but if looking good is a source of stress for you, begin early. If you're going to buy something new, tuck it away so it's fresh for the actual event. Cher (IYKYK) was right when she said you shouldn't rely on mirrors to judge your outfit. She famously used Polaroids.

Bring out the flannels. Both the pj's (check) and the Christmas sheets (check).

Prepare holiday music playlists. Begin curating a playlist for holiday gatherings. There's a start for you on page 68 for cocktails and page 178 for dinner soirees.

There may be no more idyllic spot for a night of Christmas movies than this home theater Helmstetter designed, with popcorn garlands and custom candy boxes to match the room itself.

(SNOW) BOOT CAMP / **209**

NOVEMBER

Decorate! That's right. It's finally time to deck the halls . . . and not a minute too soon. Try to get the tree(s) up just after Thanksgiving so you can enjoy it for a full month.

Tie up your meal plans. Getting your Christmas menu in order early—and gathering ingredients—will lower stress levels during the Big Week.

Mail holiday cards the Monday after Thanksgiving. The early bird gets the prime fridge placement. Cards that arrive too late get lost in the shuffle.

DECEMBER

Pick up fresh greens. Just-cut garlands and boughs are everywhere in early December. (Costco often has them at affordable prices—I remove the included bows and adorn them to my liking.)

Start a list. Keep track of thank-you cards for everything you receive, including who sent what. This is handy if your brain, like mine, is made of Swiss cheese.

Enjoy! If the dull days of December are for anything, they're for cuddling up with loved ones, toasting the year at holiday parties, and making merry in the frosty air. Break out the sled, queue up the classic Christmas movies, resuscitate your favorite traditions, and enjoy every second. Merry, merry!

OPPOSITE: The secret to making the most perfect sugar cookies in the world without losing your precious marbles: buy them. These were whipped up by Colorado's brilliant Denver Cake Company.

FOLLOWING: In Saint Moritz, Switzerland, embossed leather paneling imported from a German castle feels ultra luxe to the touch. (Not planning on importing castle castoffs to your own house? Velvet throw pillows can add a similar sense of richness.)

THIS CHRISTMAS, DO YOURSELF A FAVOR AND . . .

Read "A Christmas Memory," Truman Capote's exquisite short story about a friendship between a young boy and an elderly woman.

Write a big check. If you can afford it, there's no better feeling than sending more than you think you can to a worthy charity. Mine is Save the Children, but worthy charities abound.

Put out a seeded pine cone for the birds.

Place all your lights on a timer or plug them into an outlet attachment that can be controlled by remote. They're Santa's little helpers. It's so nice to schlep home from the office to twinkles . . . and know that they'll turn off just after you head to downy slumber.

Watch *The Shop Around the Corner*. Before *You've Got Mail*, there was James "Jimmy" Stewart and Margaret Sullavan.

— THE WAY YOU SPEND CHRISTMAS IS FAR MORE IMPORTANT THAN HOW MUCH.

—HENRY DAVID THOREAU

Acknowledgments

Sometimes the best gift is a person who comes into your life when you really need them. I have had hundreds of those, and by grace, they keep on coming. Thank you so much to one of the greatest: Juree Sondker, my editor at Gibbs Smith—indeed the entire Gibbs Smith team. Y'all get me, and I adore you! To Amy Sly and Ryan Thomann—you listened without judgment when I said I wanted this book to look like Brooke Shields' eyebrows, and I am forever grateful for the beauty you whip out of thin air. To the photographers who have perfectly captured the magic of the season and shared it with us here, I can't thank you enough. And to the designers who have so generously shared their work, you are the very definition of merry and chic.

Finally, thank you to all my parents for working so hard to create Christmas magic in my childhood. It worked. To my husband, James—the best holiday co-pilot a girl could have—you were right to propose on Christmas in Rome all those years ago. And to our perfect son, Guy: You're the best gift of all.

BUY GUIDE

Anthropologie: For all things charming, this is the mothership.

Astier de Villatte: Paris on a plate.

Costco: The place to scoop up baking supplies, Irish butter, British cheeses, and affordable fresh garlands and wreaths.

eBay: You can find fantastic antique hotel and collegiate silverware on eBay, but you'll have to fight me for it.

Etsy: My go-to for custom anything, from letterpress stationery to sugar cookies.

Facebook Marketplace: Deals, deals, deals on your neighbor's decor. I do Venmo payments and quick porch pickups if I trust the seller.

Julia Amory: Hand-blocked tablecloths and napkins in rich colorways.

Mark and Graham: Monogram addicts flock here for a reason.

McCarty's Pottery: When I was nineteen, I was sitting on William Faulkner's lap—a statue seated on a bench in Oxford, Mississippi—when a woman in a big hat walked by and said, "He would have looooved you. I know because I knew him." My obsession with Southern artists was firmly cemented then and there. McCarty's Pottery uses delta clay and has since Faulkner himself allowed them to use the earth at Rowan Oak.

Paloma & Co.: Texas designer Paloma Contreras has an incredible eye for pieces that are modern and classic at once. Love the tumblers and trays especially.

Pentreath & Hall: A British cult brand with Morris & Co. collaborations sure to stand the test of time.

The Six Bells: If Brooklyn and Stars Hollow had a baby, this would be it. Great spiral candles and serving dishes.

Talmaris, Paris: Take my money.

PAGE 215: By layering the heights of her tabletop trees and candles, Courtney Davey created a de facto skyline for the eye to wander.

PAGE 216: Rhudy's flourish of tabletop flowers has the same cheerful fizz as champagne.

PREVIOUS: Sleigh bells, bows and a graceful arch of magnolia leaves lend a very warm welcome at Parkey's door.

OPPOSITE: At Christmastime, there is no tabletop surface that fresh flowers in a mint julep cup (this one in Francis and Fabbri's home) can't improve.

PHOTO CREDITS

Tramont Ana/Shutterstock.com: 176
Maryna Auramchuk/iStockPhoto.com: 135
Brian Bieder: 39, 106
Natalia Bolotina/Shutterstock.com: 7, 12, 15, 50, 53, 58, 80, 83, 120, 123, 140, 143, 146, 156, 184, 187, 198, 201
Usa Bunjongjad/Shutterstock.com: 2, 126
Aybala Cakmakcioglu/Shutterstock.com: 2, 5, 68, 154, 172, 194
Chamomile_Olya/Shutterstock.com: 136
Marina Datsenko/Shutterstock.com: 58
Courtney Davey: 74–75, 119, 215
Kip Dawkins: 28–31, 78–79, 94–97, 114–115, 130
Makenzie Evans: 104–105, 180–183, 219, 223
Kirsten Francis: 46–49, 179, 202–207, 220
Angela George: Cover Art
HardtIllustrations/Shutterstock.com: 2, 114, 130
Brent Hofacker/Shutterstock.com: 178
Justin L. Jordan: 44–45, 54, 92–93, 127, 132, 134
Stephen Karlisch: 71
KG_design/Shutterstock.com: 165
Francesco Lagnese/OTTO: 16–19, 36, 57, 192, 201
LilaloveDesign/Shutterstock.com: 26, 224
Andy Magee/Shutterstock.com: 72, 166

Katie Mangold Photography: 32–33, 107
Rachel Alyse Manning: 66–67
maradon 333/Shutterstock.com: 37, 41, 103, 113, 129, 151, 169, 175, 202, 209, 214, 217, 218
Anna Markina/Shutterstock.com: 138
Mochuelo/Shutterstock.com: 193
Heather Nan: 90–91
Kathryn O'Shea–Evans: 144–177, 188–191, 211
Dustin Peck: 69, 110
Eric Piasecki/OTTO: 6, 15, 20–23, 83
pq189/iStockPhoto.com: 128
Annie Schlechter: 53, 84, 98–99, 123–124, 197
Annie Schlechter/The Interior Archive: 139
Emily Sewell: 26, 108–109
Andy Shell/Shutterstock.com: 196
Julie Soefer: 10, 11, 24–25, 76–77, 100–101, 143
solarus/Shutterstock.com: 183
Laura Steffan: 34–35, 38, 72, 112, 216
Steve Steinhardt: 86–89, 111, 116–118, 133, 187, 208–209
tofutyklein/Shutterstock.com: 148
Vivite/Shutterstock.com: 137
Simon Upton/The Interior Archive: 212-213
Bert VanderVeen: 40–43, 60–65, 102

OPPOSITE: In Parkey's home, even the pooch gets a custom stocking.

ABOUT THE AUTHOR

Colorado-based writer Kathryn O'Shea-Evans is the author of *Alpine Style* (also published by Gibbs Smith), and writes regularly for *The Wall Street Journal*, *The Washington Post*, and *Architectural Digest*. She runs a holiday decor company, Aspen Grange, in her spare time, and believes it's never too early to decorate for Christmas.